# Confronting an "Axis of Cyber"?

## China, Iran, North Korea, Russia in Cyberspace

edited by Fabio Rugge

ISPI

Via Alamanni, 11 – 20141 Milano – Italy
www.ledizioni.it
info@ledizioni.it

CONFRONTING AN "AXIS OF CYBER"? CHINA, IRAN, NORTH KOREA, RUSSIA IN CYBERSPACE
Edited by Fabio Rugge
First edition: October 2018

*Published with the support of the Italian Ministry of Foreign Affairs and International Cooperation.*
*The opinions expressed are those of the authors. They do not reflect the opinions or views of ISPI or the Italian Ministry of Foreign Affairs and International Cooperation.*

Print ISBN 9788867058655
ePub ISBN 9788867058662
Pdf ISBN 9788867058679
DOI 10.14672/67058655

ISPI. Via Clerici, 5
20121, Milano
www.ispionline.it

Catalogue and reprints information: www.ledizioni.it

# Table of Contents

# Introduction

The year 2018 marks the thirtieth anniversary of the Morris worm, the first malware ever released in the Internet. Thirty years later, technological innovations have dramatically increased the importance of the Internet in virtually every economic, social and political endeavor, tremendously expanding the potential "surface" of cyber attacks. The cyber domain makes it possible to gather privileged information, disrupt industrial processes, create havoc by targeting, for instance, ICT supporting critical infrastructures, and to launch cyber-enabled information warfare campaigns against largely unaware foreign target audiences. Cyberspace, in sum, allows states to achieve strategic results with campaigns that fall below the threshold of the "use of force", while offering an unprecedented level of plausible deniability, as the real perpetrator of a cyber attack is always difficult to identify with certainty. And yet, this is only the beginning: we are in the midst of a digital revolution. By 2025, with the development of the Internet of Things (IoT), the cyber domain will connect more than 75 billion devices, many of which will control key functions of our daily lives and most of our critical infrastructures.

As such, the cyber domain has already become, and will increasingly be, too important for national security not to be also the arena where national interests naturally collide. This, in fact, happens more and more frequently, as demonstrated by the recurrent examples of international crises originating from states' behaviours in cyberspace. This is why the Italian

Institute of International Political Studies (ISPI) decided last year to create its Centre on Cybersecurity. The aim is to analyse the dynamics occurring in cyberspace and their growing impact on international relations.

In this first Report from the Centre, the focus will be on the ongoing confrontation between states in cyberspace, and on the worrisome distrust developing within the international community with regard to the objectives pursued by states in cyberspace. In particular, taking stock of the accusations that US administrations consistently put forward in virtually every strategic document released in recent years concerning the behaviour displayed in cyberspace by China, North Korea, Russia and Iran, this volume draws a provocative link between the current grouping of these four countries and the concept of the "axis of evil" adopted by the Bush administration in the aftermath of the terrorist attacks of 9/11. In this sense, the Report investigates the behaviour, motivations and capabilities of China, North Korea, Russia and Iran in the cyber domain, and highlights the current irreconcilable political cleavage between these four countries and the West in their respective approaches "in and around" cyberspace. Even though every state uses cyberspace to protect and advance its national interests in the global cyber arena, these four countries appear, in the Western perspective, to have chosen cyberspace as the "domain of choice" for pursuing a destabilising strategic effect in "the real world", insidiously leveraging the inherent difficulty in attributing cyber attacks. But there is an even more fundamental reason why the two approaches seem destined to clash, possibly justifying – in this limited sense – the perception that the West is confronted with some sort of an "Axis 2.0" upholding a radically different set of principles and values from the ones that shape the Western perception of the Internet – and, ultimately, of the world. While autocratic regimes consider a free and open Internet an intrinsic threat to their grip on power, the West – notwithstanding the intrinsic vulnerabilities of its "open societies" – considers the Internet a "global common" where centuries-old battles over human rights and individual freedoms are now playing out, a domain that must be protected against national constraints hidden under the banner of "national security".

As highlighted in the introductory chapter by Fabio Rugge, the editor of this report, the current confrontation in cyberspace is translating, at the international level, into a massive "security paradox", because the cyber strategies and capabilities developed by each state to defend national security may be perceived as – and, to some extent, are – offensive in character, thus undermining trust within the international community. In this security environment, international stability becomes volatile, the risk of escalations of the conflict in the conventional domain becomes increasingly concrete, and the international balance of power more and more difficult to assess and maintain. And yet, this unpredictable international order appears to be the best achievable so far, considering how sovereign nations will inevitably try to attain their respective cyber superiority. In order to fully grasp these apparently irreconcilable conceptualizations of cyberspace, it is useful to look at the empirical dimension of the countries that comprise the so-called "Axis of Cyber". The volume looked at two main elements of their cyber approaches: their cyber capabilities and known cyber campaigns. Although it is very difficult to understand "what is really going on" in cyberspace and to rely on a certain attribution of responsibility for cyber attacks, a lot of information is available, and a common understanding is developing about each international actor's motivations and behaviour.

Russia has been, within the so-called "axis", one of the most active actors in the cyber arena. The cyber campaigns that may be traced more or less directly to Moscow, starting from the one originating in 2007 from its territory and directed against Estonia up to the more recent one against the Democratic National Committee in the US, brought worldwide public attention to cybersecurity issues. In their chapter, Tim Maurer and Garrett Hinck underline that Russia's approach to cyberspace has been deeply shaped by its Soviet Union past, in particular from the information war fought – and lost – against the West. Since the mid-1990s the Kremlin has been conducting a diplomatic campaign for cyberspace regulation at the international level, a regulation that, in its intention, should safeguard the "information space" against the threat of foreign interference. The United States, however, has always been against such an approach. While Moscow has been building a strong apparatus to control and manage the Internet available to its citizens within its borders, it has also exploited this domain to pursue its strategic interests globally. To achieve its goals, Russia appears to have successfully developed technological capabilities and a particular informal public-private partnership with the hacker community.

The Russian approach has been in part emulated by other countries sharing the same concern for their stability, threatened by foreign influence through the Internet – or, in Western perception, by a free, open and global Internet. One above all is China. As analysed by Dean Cheng, the informational aspect of cyberspace is vital for Beijing. As such, Chinese authorities began to pay attention to information technologies beginning in 1980. Through the decades, the People's Republic of China (PRC) has developed an impressive ability to filter and control communication both across its borders and within its polity. Along with the creation of the so-called "Great Firewall of China", which is an instrument to keep unauthorised information from spreading in the country, PRC authorities proposed at the international level the concept of Internet sovereignty, which is a strategic issue for Beijing. Without obtaining results, Chinese authorities keep on isolating the domestic Internet community from the rest of the world.

A similar state control on cyberspace has been developed by North Korea, which for more than three decades has been building an impressive mechanism to restrict access to the global Internet. Pyongyang, as explained by Daniel A. Pinkston, despite its international isolation, has been very attentive to technological developments and spent financial and human resources to catch up with the rest of the world. China and Russia are strategic partners as they provide Internet connection to the country. North Korea made news headlines on multiple occasions for its cyber-attacks around the world, such as the cyber-attack against Sony Pictures Entertainment in 2014 and the creation and release of the WannaCry ransomware in 2017.

Last but not least among the group of countries that may form an "axis reloaded" and challenge Western interests through cyberspace there is Iran. Lior Tabansky underlines how Iran may be tempted to undermine the Western-led international system by using proxies and engaging in hostilities below the threshold of armed warfare. Cyber-attacks are a perfect tool to attain such a goal. In his chapter, Tabansky argues that Iran has successfully conducted several cyber campaigns to the detriment of the West and points to the absence of any retaliation against Teheran.

It is possible to build two main arguments out of these cases. First of all, by analysing the new type of conflicts in the "fifth domain", it is possible to argue that the classical concepts used in warfare do not work the same way in cyberspace. For example, the idea of deterrence – which was one of the main strategic elements ensuring some stability during the Cold War – is clearly not straightforwardly adaptable to the cyber arena. Indeed, Umberto Gori argues that because of the intrinsic characteristics of cyberspace, the classical perception of power, which drives states' behaviours in the international arena, has limited applicability in the digital domain. Therefore, a balance of power in cyberspace would be hard to achieve.

The second argument derives from the nature of cyberspace, which is on the one hand the "domain of ambiguity" and, on the other, anarchic as rules are still in the making and states cannot rely on well-known and shared practices used in the kinetic domain. Therefore, defining rules for state behaviours is an absolute priority, especially when it comes to the use of force and coercion in cyberspace. As discussed by James Lewis, attempts at the international level have been made but they left important issues unresolved. The absence of clear norms may ultimately lead, in the context of renewed international tensions, to a rapid escalation with potential dramatic "real world" implications.

As highlighted in the Report, a hypothetical "Axis of Cyber" might be confirmed only as a mirror image of the ongoing international tensions, and as a reflection of the harsher and harsher confrontation taking place in cyberspace. Naming and shaming specific countries might prove to be an effective strategy to raise international awareness about the risk inherent in the profound political cleavages playing out "in and around" cyberspace, and to reinforce the notion of what is to be considered permissible state behaviour in cyberspace. However, from the analytical point of view, if we want to try to grasp the complexity of the developments underway in the cyber arena and their growing impact on international security, a much more in-depth analysis needs to be developed. This Report is an effort to that end.

*Giampiero Massolo*
*ISPI President*

# 1. An "Axis" Reloaded?

Fabio Rugge

Threat assessments of intelligence communities worldwide are unambiguous: the Internet is being militarised[1]. States are continuously pursuing strategic goals with sophisticated cyber campaigns that fall under the threshold of the "use of force", and the risks of misperceptions, misunderstanding and conventional escalations following cyber attacks are increasing. The "first web war" was waged against Estonia in 2007: a massive distributed denial of service attack (DDoS) was launched from the Russian territory (although the involvement of the Russian government has never proved) and paralysed the country for days. Even if the attack was labelled as a "cyber riot" rather than a military attack, its political, military and strategic implications were clear: cyberspace had been used to achieve actual results "on the ground".

2018 marks the tenth anniversary of the first use of cyber attacks in support of kinetic military operations, during the Georgian War: a new era in military affairs began. Since then, examples of cyber attacks during international crisis and military operations have multiplied: the Stuxnet worm (2010) that

[1] "We recognise that adversaries already condemn US efforts to defend our interests and allies as aggressive, and we expect they will similarly seek to portray our strategy as "militarising" the cyberspace domain. The Command makes no apologies for defending US interests as directed by the President through the Secretary of Defense in a domain already militarised by our adversaries", Achieve and Maintain Cyberspace Superiority. Command Vision for US Cyber Command, 23 March 2018, p. 10.

targeted Iranian centrifuges for the enrichment of uranium, the cyber attack against the Ukrainian power grids in the Ukrainian war (2015), the hacking of the Qatari news agency during the recent Gulf crisis (2017).

The event that probably serves as the titular event in cybersecurity and cyber-enabled information warfare (CEIW) in the headlines of the Western world is Russia's meddling in the 2016 US presidential elections' public debate. The US Intelligence community assesses with "high confidence" that Russia's military intelligence (GRU) gained access to the Democratic National Committee (DNC) computer networks in July 2015, and maintained it until at least June 2016. By May, Russia's Intelligence had exfiltrated large volumes of data from the DNC. Someone under the name of "Guccifer 2.0" subsequently leaked to Wikileaks.com and DCLeaks.com the material stolen from DNC. The scandal that followed was exploited by a massive CEIW campaign to discredit Hillary Clinton and, more importantly, to erode trust in US institutions.

Yet this does not seem to raise the public's understanding of the true nature of cyber threats and of the potential impact on international security of the ongoing confrontation in cyberspace. The low level of public awareness is understandable, but worrisome. Cyberspace is the "domain of ambiguity", where high-end threats operate in the same environment sharing many of the technical features of low-level skirmishes and criminal activities. In this domain, it is impossible to understand and anticipate the motivation and the scope of a cyber campaign without considering the strategic, political and operational context in which it occurs. The difficulty in attributing the cyber attacks, together with the widespread re-course in cyberspace to false flag computer network operations, make it difficult to know "what is really going on" in the cyber domain, and to make a sense out of it. National intelligence communities usually are better placed and equipped to handle sensible information and grasp the complexity "behind the curtains" of the ongoing confrontation in the cyber domain – but this is also another reason why an in-depth understanding of cyber affairs is not easily accessible to the general public.

Technological innovation, moreover, is transforming our societies at a pace that public opinions and policymakers are unable to keep up with, as it takes time and a deep cultural change in order to adapt to the new dynamics brought by the Internet. Technological innovation seems to be the primary driver of social change, while politics appears, if not incapable of having a real impact on the future, at least certainly not in the driver seat. While we cannot envision a future without the Internet, it is almost as complicated to picture what kind of Internet we will share in the future. The impact of new technologies on our professional, private and social life are hard to foresee what will be, but what we do know is that the cyber domain and the "real world" continue to be increasingly intertwined. What kind of Internet we will have is therefore an issue that regards us very closely: our freedom and our security will depend more and more on how free and secure our Internet remains.

## The Usual Suspects

The threat of foreign interference in the United States elections through unauthorised access to election and campaign infrastructure or the covert distribution of propaganda and disinformation features very high on the US political agenda that President Trump signed in September, in preparations of the 2018 Midterm elections, an executive order[2] "on Imposing Certain Sanctions in the Event of Foreign Interference in a United States Election". The President confirms that "[i]n recent years, the proliferation of digital devices and Internet-based communications has created significant vulnerabilities and magnified the scope and intensity of the threat of foreign interference.

---

[2] The executive order is available at: White House, Executive Order on Imposing Certain Sanctions in the Event of Foreign Interference in a United States Election, Foreign Policy, 12 September 2018.

The threat of Russia's information warfare features prominently also in the National Security Strategy[3] of the United States, released in December 2017, where it is stated that "[A]merica's competitors weaponise information to attack the values and institutions that underpin free societies, while shielding themselves from outside information. [...] Russia uses information operations as part of its offensive cyber efforts to influence public opinion across the globe". Likewise, the Worldwide Threat Assessment of the US Intelligence Community, released last March, draws the attention on the expected surge in Russia's offensive operations in cyberspace:

> [w]e expect that Russia will conduct bolder and more disruptive cyber operations during the next year, most likely using new capabilities against Ukraine. The Russian Government is likely to build on the wide range of operations it is already conducting, including disruption of Ukrainian energy-distribution networks, hack-and-leak influence operations, distributed denial-of-service attacks, and false flag operations. In the next year, Russian intelligence and security services will continue to probe US and allied critical infrastructures, as well as target the United States, NATO, and allies for insights into US policy.

Russia is the main player but is not the only state on the bench. Iran, North Korea and China are also consistently indicated in Western intelligence assessments and official statements as the main actors of direct or state-sponsored offensive campaigns in or through cyberspace"[4]. The US National Cyber Security

[3] White House, National Security Strategy of the United States of America, December 2017, pp. 34-35.

[4]As the Worldwide Threat Assessment of the US Intelligence Community confirms, "Russia, China, Iran, and North Korea will pose the greatest cyber threats to the United States during the next year. These states are using cyber operations as a low-cost tool of statecraft, and we assess that they will work to use cyber operations to achieve strategic objectives unless they face clear repercussions for their cyber operations. [...] The use of cyber attacks as a foreign policy tool outside of military conflict has been mostly limited to sporadic lower-level attacks. Russia, Iran, and North Korea, however, are testing more aggressive

Strategy, released in September 2018 by the White House[5], names only these four countries, and affirms that they "conducted reckless cyber attacks that harmed American and international businesses and our allies and partners without paying costs likely to deter future cyber aggression. China engaged in cyber-enabled economic espionage and trillions of dollars of intellectual property theft". According to the latest US Command Vision for US Cyber Command[6]

> Russia, China, Iran, and North Korea invest in military capabilities that reduce our military's competitive advantages and compromise our national security. Some of these states have demonstrated the resolve, technical capability, and persistence to undertake strategic cyberspace campaigns, including theft of intellectual property and personally identifiable information that are vital to our defences. Disruptive technologies will eventually accelerate our adversaries' ability to impose costs.

These accusations seem to be confirmed also by the Computer Security Incidents Response Teams and private companies in cybersecurity business. According to the July Incident Response Threat Report of the cybersecurity company Carbon Black[7], for instance, incident response professionals assess that "the vast majority of cyber attacks originate from two nation-states: Russia and China. […] Nation-states such as Russia, China, Iran and North Korea are actively operationalising and supporting technologically advanced cyber militias". Carbon Black's chief cybersecurity officer went even further, maintaining that, in his

---

cyber attacks that pose growing threats to the United States and US partners". Worldwide Threat Assessment of the US Intelligence Community, Statement of the Record, Daniel R. Coats, Director of General Intelligence, 6 March 2018, p. 5.

[5] White House, National Cyber Strategy of the United States of America, September 2018, p. 20.

[6] Achieve and Maintain Cyberspace Superiority. Command Vision for US Cyber Command…, cit., p. 3.

[7] *Quarterly Incident Response Threat*, Carbon Back Report, July 2018, downloaded on 8 September 2018.

opinion, Russia, China and North Korea have an unwritten operational agreement not to target each other: "[n]one of these three will hack the others, and at the same time they are benefitting from each other's colonisation of wide swathes of the West".

However, Russia, China, Iran and North Korea are not alone in engaging in cyber campaigns. Thousands of highly classified documents leaked in 2013 by the former US government contractor Edward Snowden showed that also the United States was developing cyber defensive and offensive capabilities in order to enhance its relative cyber power, which can be defined as "the ability to use cyberspace to create advantages and influence events in other operational environments and across the instruments of power"[8]. All members of the international community regularly engage in the collection of valuable intelligence, even through computer network operations and signal intelligence support to cyber defence (SSCD) – after all, these are all endeavours not forbidden by international law. This because cyber power is an essential component of contemporary sovereignty[9], and it is a legitimate goal for every state to strengthen all dimensions of its sovereign power. In a security environment in which "it is undeniable that homeland is no longer a sanctuary"[10], the use

[8] D.T. Kuehl, "From Cyberspace to Cyberpower: Defining the Problem," in F.D. Kramer, S. Starr and L.K. Wentz (eds.), *Cyberpower and National Security*, Washington D.C., National Defense University Press, Potomac Books, 2009, quoted and adopted by Prof. Joseph S. Nye Jr in his *Cyber Power*, Belfer Center for Science and International Affairs, Harvard Kennedy School, May 2010.

[9] "Cyberspace will no longer be treated as a separate category of policy or activity disjointed from other elements of national power. The United States will integrate the employment of cyber options across every element of national power", National Cyber Strategy of the United States of America…, cit., p. 20.

[10] Summary of the National Defense Strategy of the United States of America, 2018, p. 3, "It is now undeniable that the homeland is no longer a sanctuary. America is a target, whether from terrorists seeking to attack our citizens; malicious cyber activity against personal, commercial, or government infrastructure; or political and information subversion. New threats to commercial and military uses of space are emerging, while increasing digital connectivity of all aspects of life, business, government, and military creates significant vulnerabilities. During

of cyber power is essential in enhancing national security. In this sense, cyberspace is simply a new domain in which the never-ending international confrontation takes place[11], with the noteworthy difference that it is a "domain of ambiguity" where geographical frontiers are irrelevant, actors are largely unknown, civilian assets are often the main targets, and the rules of states' behaviour are difficult to identify, tough to establish and almost impossible to enforce.

Establishing clear norms of acceptable behaviour in cyberspace and deterring malicious cyber campaign is hard enough among states, but it could prove futile against non-state actors. If, in today's security environment, non-states actors may play a destabilising impact on the traditional Westphalian international order, this is especially so in cyberspace, where it is common for David to defeat Goliaths. Non-state actors[12] extensively profit of the relative impunity that characterise cyberspace, of its low barriers to entry[13] and of the relatively easy endeavour of finding vulnerabilities in information, communications and technology (ICT) networks[14]. The use

conflict, attacks against our critical defence, government, and economic infrastructure must be anticipated".

[11] "Challenges to United States security and economic interests, from nation states and other groups, which have long existed in the offline world are now increasingly occurring in cyberspace", National Cyber Strategy of the United States of America…, cit., p. 20.

[12] "Today, cyberspace offers state and non-state actors the ability to wage campaigns against American political, economic, and security interests without ever physically crossing our borders. Cyber attacks offer adversaries low-cost and deniable opportunities to seriously damage or disrupt critical infrastructure, cripple American businesses, weaken our Federal networks, and attack the tools and devices that Americans use every day to communicate and conduct business", National Security Strategy of the United States of America…, cit., p. 12.

[13] "[B]arriers to entry in the cyber domain are so low that non-state actors and small states can play significant roles at low levels of cost", J.S. Nye Jr, (2010), p. 15.

[14] "Efforts to deter state and non-state actors alike are also hindered by the fact that, despite significant public and private investments in cybersecurity, finding and exploiting cyber vulnerabilities remains relatively easy. Those defending networks must be near perfect in their efforts, while malicious cyber

of cyber weapons by terrorists, for instance, is a likely – and extremely upsetting – development, especially considering how easy is to acquire in the dark web the knowledge necessary to attack enemies' networks, or even ready-to-use cyber weapons. Moreover, transnational cybercrime organisations are very relevant actors of cyberspace, as they are among the most significant world investors in research and development of always-new offensive capabilities, and they therefore actively contribute to the international cyber arms proliferation. Cybercrime syndicates, moreover, are difficult to eradicate because of their economic power and because dismantling physical assets does not solve the problem, as malicious actors may access the Internet from everywhere in the world. Furthermore, police and judicial cooperation is complicated by the difficulty in attributing the attack (especially since this would typically involve sharing intelligence sources and findings), and criminals are known to be available to act on behalf of states seeking plausible deniability through non-sovereign proxies[15]. Terrorists and criminals are probably the most dangerous actors of a domain which is in fact characterised by its great diversity: hackers and the cyber underground, hacktivists, companies and private online individuals may all contribute to make security volatile in cyberspace while they seek to advance their multiple military, political and financial interests.

So why, if "everybody hacks", is the conduct in cyberspace of Russia, North Korea, China and Iran any different from that of the United States – or any other country, for that matter? Is the US applying a double standard when it comes to define the behaviour in cyberspace of these four countries?

---

actors may only need to find a single vulnerability to gain a foothold in a network", "Recommendations to the President on Deterring Adversaries and Better Protecting the American People from Cyber Threats", US Department of State, Office of the Coordinator for Cyber Issues, 31 May 2018, p. 2.

[15] T. Maurer, *Cyber Mercenaries. The State, Hackers, and Power*, Cambridge, Cambridge University Press, 2018.

Are they really a new "axis of evil"[16] – only, this time, operating in and through cyberspace?[17]

## Points of Views and Values

There are at least two perspectives that explain why Russia, North Korea, China and Iran are lumped together when describing their behaviours and approaches to the cyber domain. The first one has to do with the interests these actors try to pursue engaging in cyberspace campaigns. Even though "everybody hacks", there is a great deal of difference between monitoring global networks to protect national ICT assets and to disrupt terrorist plots, and using cyber weapons to advance

[16] The notorious definitions of an "axis of evil" – echoing the Rome-Berlin-Tokyo "Axis" of the II World War – was introduced on the occasion of the State of the Union Address delivered by George W. Bush in 2002, in the aftermath of the 9/11 attacks. The President accused Iraq, Iran, and North Korea of being the main supporters of terrorism and of seeking WMD, and held that "States like these and their terrorist allies constitute an axis of evil, arming to threaten the peace of the world. By seeking weapons of mass destruction, these regimes pose a grave and growing danger". The notion was repeatedly used during Mr. Bush presidency, and even expanded in a speech delivered at The Heritage Foundation a few months later by the then Under Secretary of State for Arms Control and International Security – and today's National Security Advisor – John Bolton, whom argued that the threat of WMD was emerging even from states beyond the three of the axis mentioned by President Bush, to include Libya, Syria and Cuba, and promised that the US would "take all necessary measures" to eliminate terrorist threats from these countries.

[17] "If the first 15 years of the 21st century were defined by the so-called Axis of Evil – the phrase George W. Bush applied to Iraq, Iran, and North Korea in the days after 9/11 for their support of terrorists – the next 15 years will likely be defined by the Access of Evil, as state and non-state cyber terrorists use technology to bypass our defences in ways that damage businesses, lives, and nations. There is little question about the charter members of this club. As Texas Congressman Michael McCaul, the Chairman of the House Committee on Homeland Security, recently put it, "Russia, China, North Korea and Iran are increasingly hacking into U.S. companies and government networks for espionage purposes or financial gain", S. Weiss, "Moving from Axis to Access of Evil", *Huffpost*, the Blog, 8 April 2015.

destabilising geo-strategic interests through hostile targeting of foreign ICT assets (most of the times civilian) and conducting CEIW to taint the most sensible democratic processes.

In this respect, Russia, North Korea, China and Iran stand out because they all appear as having elected cyberspace the "domain of choice" to pursue their geo-strategic objectives aggressively. Leveraging the asymmetric advantage intrinsic in computer network operations and showing an audacity justified only by the impunity that characterises cyberspace – "with a recklessness they would never consider in other domains"[18]. In this perspective, the accusations against Russia, North Korea, China and Iran have little to do with their cyber capabilities as such, but focus instead on the destabilising effects that these capabilities serve "in the real world", such as undermining the democratic electoral processes through CEIW, stealing the intellectual property for attaining an unfair market advantage, targeting the cyber components supporting critical infrastructure in order to intimidate and deter, and exfiltrating privileged information from political enemies in order to blackmail them[19].

---

[18] "The Administration recognises that the United States is engaged in a continuous competition against strategic adversaries, rogue states, and terrorist and criminal networks. Russia, China, Iran, and North Korea all use cyberspace as a means to challenge the United States, its allies, and partners, often with a recklessness they would never consider in other domains. These adversaries use cyber tools to undermine our economy and democracy, steal our intellectual property, and sow discord in our democratic processes. We are vulnerable to peacetime cyber attacks against critical infrastructure, and the risk is growing that these countries will conduct cyber attacks against the United States during a crisis short of war. These adversaries are continually developing new and more effective cyber weapons", National Cyber Strategy of the United States of America…, cit., pp. 2-3.

[19] The US National Cyber Strategy goes further, saying that "Our competitors and adversaries […] benefit from the open Internet, while constricting and controlling their own people's access to it, and actively undermine the principles of an open Internet in international forums. They hide behind notions of sovereignty while recklessly violating the laws of other states by engaging in pernicious economic espionage and malicious cyber activities, causing significant economic disruption and harm to individuals, commercial and non-commercial

The other reason why Russia, North Korea, China and Iran are seen as an "Axis 2.0" is their irreconcilable approach towards the Internet compared to the Western democracies. "The United States Government", in the words of the National Cyber Strategy of September 2018, "conceptualises Internet freedom as the online exercise of human rights and fundamental freedoms – such as the freedoms of expression, association, peaceful assembly, religion or belief, and privacy rights online – regardless of frontiers or medium. By extension, Internet freedom also supports the free flow of information online that enhances international trade and commerce, fosters innovation, and strengthens both national and international security. As such, United States Internet freedom principles (sic) are inextricably linked to our national security"[20]. While the West believes that "centuries-old battles over human rights and fundamental freedoms are now playing out online"[21], autocratic regimes view the Internet as a threat to their grip on power, and social media servers located outside of the government's control as an intrinsic risk to their survival. They will not be able to concede freedom over the Internet to their citizens, and are actively involved in controlling the Internet's traffic. If, in an international law perspective, these differences of approach are inherent in the principles of sovereignty and even protected by the principle of domestic jurisdiction, from the point of view of human rights and civil liberties they cannot be put at the same level: autocratic regimes are engaged in limiting the

interests, and governments across the world. They view cyberspace as an arena where the United States' overwhelming military, economic, and political power could be neutralised and where the United States and its allies and partners are vulnerable", Ibid., p. 1.

[20] Ibid., pp. 24-25.

[21] Ibid., p. 24. It is worth noting that, while to today's eyes it may seem maybe a little naïve, at the beginning of the cyber age many hoped that the global Internet could finally give voice to humanity without the deforming lens of national interests: see, for instance, the notorious J.P. Barlow, A Declaration of the Independence of Cyberspace, Electronic Frontier Foundation (EFF), Davos, Switzerland, 8 February 1996.

free flow of ideas and restricting fundamental individual liberties, while the West is engaged in enforcing what it perceives as a global common where individual liberties may flourish. It is not a surprise, therefore, that Russia, North Korea, China and Iran perceive Internet's freedom as a Western attempt to undermine their domestic stability, and claim that the United States and the West have been, and are, actively involved in implementing online information campaigns in order to influence the course of a series of regime change over the last two decades (for instance the "Colour Revolutions" and the "Arab Springs"). The West, on the other hand, intends to protect the inherent vulnerabilities of open societies by ensuring that autocratic regimes avoid exploiting them in order to achieve international strategic advantage, and takes pride in being accountable to its own public opinions and electorates. The difference is so fundamental that it will hardly ever be possible to reconcile the two different approaches playing out in cyberspace. In this limited sense[22], this profound cultural and political cleavage justifies the Western perception that we are, in fact, confronted with some sort of an "axis 2.0", who embraces principles and values that are radically alternative to the ones that shape our perception of the Internet – and, in sum, of the world[23]. Significantly,

---

[22] On this account, Professor Joseph Nye observes: "There is nothing today like the infamous Axis of Nazi Germany and its allies in the 1930s. While Russia and China are both authoritarian and find it useful to caucus against the US in international bodies like the United Nations Security Council, they have very different interests. China is a rising power that is highly intertwined with the international economy, including the US. In contrast, Russia is a declining country with serious demographic and public health problems, with energy rather than finished goods accounting for two-thirds of its exports", J.S. Nye Jr, "Human Rights and the Fate of the Liberal Order", Project Syndacate, 17 September 2018.

[23] "[A]mericans sometimes took for granted that the supremacy of the United States in the cyber domain would remain unchallenged, and that America's vision for an open, interoperable, reliable, and secure Internet would inevitably become a reality. Americans believed the growth of the Internet would carry the universal aspirations for free expression and individual liberty around the world. *Americans assumed the opportunities to expand communication, commerce, and free exchange of ideas would be self-evident.* Large parts of the world have embraced America's vision of a

even this second stance has little to do with computer network capabilities as such.

These irreconcilable political cleavages risk thrusting the "balkanisation" of the global Internet, its breakdown in national or regional networks, most likely under the banner of national security's prerogatives and of the principle of domestic jurisdiction[24]. In turn, such a development would undoubtedly pave the way for a dystopian evolution of the Internet in some regions of the world, with autocratic states affirming their authority over online content. On this path, States could soon be capable of keeping their citizens always connected, always "correctly" informed and always controlled, as only Orwell could preconise[25]. This "balkanisation" of the Internet would, in turn, nourish among public opinions divergent views of the world, contributing to make the Internet an element of division rather than of mutual understanding at the global level.

## Volatile Security

Security "in and around" cyberspace will likely remain volatile for the years to come, given the conflicting strategic national interests and the diverging cultural and ideological approaches at play. The confrontation between the West on the one hand, and Russia, North Korea, China and Iran on the other, will most likely impact international stability in profound ways. It will most likely trigger sharp escalations of hostilities in the

---

shared and open cyberspace for the mutual benefit of all. Our competitors and adversaries, however, have taken an opposite approach", National Cyber Strategy of the United States of America…, cit., p. 1 (italic mine).

[24] "We will work to ensure that our approach to an open Internet is the international standard. We will also work to prevent authoritarian states that view the open Internet as a political threat from transforming the free and open Internet into an authoritarian web under their control, under the guise of security or countering terrorism", Ibid., p. 24.

[25] On this issue, A. Klimburg, *The Darkening Web. The War To Cyberspace*, Penguin Press, 2017.

conventional domain, the adoption of international countermeasures in response to cyber campaigns[26], and the application of conflicting operational standards concerning the Internet development. Technological developments in the fields of Artificial Intelligence, the Internet of Things, robotics and quantum computing (to name just a few) will most likely consolidate the current trends, and the international community will drift – as explained in detail by Professor Umberto Gori in his chapter of this Report – towards a Balance of Power that is much more difficult to assess and to maintain[27].

In this scenario of ambiguity and uncertainty, every state is actively engaged in attaining "cyber superiority", defined as the "degree of dominance in cyberspace by one force that permits the secure, reliable conduct of operations by that force, and its related land, air, maritime, and space forces at a given time and place without prohibitive interference by an adversary"[28]. Cyber superiority is key in enhancing situational awareness and attribution, allowing countries under attack to impose swift, costly and transparent consequences in response to malicious behaviour[29]. Cyber superiority is also vital in mapping the the-

[26] "All instruments of national power are available to prevent, respond to, and deter malicious cyber activity against the United States. This includes diplomatic, information, military (both kinetic and cyber), financial, intelligence, public attribution, and law enforcement capabilities", National Cyber Strategy of the United States of America…, cit., p. 21.

[27] "This now-persistent engagement in cyberspace is already altering the strategic balance of power", Ibid., p. 20.

[28] Achieve and Maintain Cyberspace Superiority. Command Vision for US Cyber Command…, cit., p. 6.

[29] "All instruments of national power are available to prevent, respond to, and deter malicious cyber activity against the United States. This includes diplomatic, information, military (both kinetic and cyber), financial, intelligence, public attribution, and law enforcement capabilities. The United States will formalise and make routine how we work with like-minded partners to attribute and deter malicious cyber activities with integrated strategies that impose swift, costly, and transparent consequences when malicious actors harm the United States or our partners", National Cyber Strategy of the United States of America…, cit., p. 21. Commenting the new National Cyber Strategy, Christopher Painter,

atre of future conflicts, in anticipating the adversary's vulnerabilities and in contesting its courses of action, and in establishing the deterrence posture – which is particularly complex to establish in cyberspace, as actionable attribution, and therefore retaliation, are troublesome[30]. If the new US (and, hopefully, Western) posture will succeed in enhancing predictability in cyberspace, the international community might then be facilitated in agreeing on constraining rules of behaviour, and in enhancing international cooperation against non-state malicious actors.

The problem with these developments is that the national legitimate quests for cyber superiority translate, at the international level, in a massive security paradox ("my security is your insecurity") that undermines trust within the international community and threatens international stability. In fact, one of the main features of cyberspace is the fact that offensive and defensive capabilities develop "hand in hand": it is impossible to ensure the appropriate defence of national ICT networks without knowing how an attack is executed and without developing a certain degree of cyber superiority. Moreover, cyber incidents typically do not allow time to react, and therefore mapping the battlefield before full-scale hostilities erupt is an operational

---

Commissioner on the Global Commission for the Stability of Cyberspace and formerly the top cyber diplomat at the US Department of State wrote: "While we're getting better at naming and shaming some of those responsible for cyber events, that's not sufficient to deter actors like Russia or North Korea. Real consequences for bad state behaviour that will affect their decision making is still desperately lacking. That creates the 'norm' that such bad behaviour is acceptable – or at least cost free", C. Painter, "The White House cyber strategy: words must be backed by action", *The Strategist*, Australian Strategic Policy Institute, 25 September 2018.

[30] See, i.e. M. Libicki, "Would Deterrence in Cyberspace Work Even with Attribution?", *Georgetown Journal of International Affairs*, 22 April 2015; F.D. Kramer, R.J. Butler, and C. Lotrionte, "Cyber and Deterrence. The Military-Civil Nexus in High-End Conflict", Atlantic Council, Brent Scowcroft Center on International Security, January 2017; M.P. Fischerkeller and R.J. Harknett, "Deterrence is Not a Credible Strategy for Cyberspace", Foreign Policy Research Institute, Summer 2017.

imperative. This implies conducting intelligence, surveillance and reconnaissance (ISR) operations against the networks of potential enemies – operations that, in turn, may easily be perceived as military in character. Signaling about offensive capabilities, also, serves also the purpose of deterring potential enemies by clarifying the readiness to respond "in kind" to an attack[31]. How else to read, for instance, the malwares that have been found in critical infrastructures around the world, other than weapons designed and planted to indicate readiness to strike in case of full-scale hostilities? Finally, cyber weapons are inherently secret, as they rely on ICT vulnerabilities (zero-days) to be effective; as such, visibility on each other cyber arsenals is virtually impossible, an armament control regime is unsustainable, and the security paradox becomes more relevant everyday.

The United States made it clear its intention of scaling its response "to the magnitude of the threat, removing constraints on [its] speed and agility, and maneuvering to counter adversaries and enhance [its] national security"[32]. The new US defence posture in cyberspace adopts an unambiguous pro-active role against any potential source of malicious behaviour in cyberspace, in order to "defend forward" and to sustain the cause of international order by clarifying what is to be considered as a permissible behaviour in cyberspace. The Cyber Command's Vision argues that the previous reactive posture was conceding way too much to adversaries seeking to achieve a strategic effect with cyber campaigns under the threshold of the use of force, and every other option short of "persistent engagement" (that is, the buzz-words of the last decade: resilience, deterrence

[31] "The President already has a wide variety of cyber and non-cyber options for deterring and responding to cyber activities that constitute a use of force. Credibly demonstrating that the United States is capable of imposing significant costs on those who carry out such activities is indispensable to maintaining and strengthening deterrence". Recommendations to the President on "Recommendations to the President on Deterring Adversaries and Better Protecting the American People from Cyber Threats"..., cit., p. 2.

[32] Achieve and Maintain Cyberspace Superiority. Command Vision for US Cyber Command..., cit., p. 2.

by denial, "active defence") has to be completely rethought by pro-actively engaging US adversaries wherever and whenever they are found, in order to obtain tactical, operational and strategic advantage[33]. The new US posture in the cyber domain must instead acknowledge that cyberspace is a continuously contested domain, and that an effective deterrence in cyberspace postulates a "persistent" (or, maybe more appropriately, "perpetual"[34]) engagement with the adversaries. The ultimate goal of the current US Cyber Command's Vision is "to improve the security and stability of cyberspace" and to avoid escalations in the conventional domain "by clarifying the distinction between acceptable and unacceptable behaviour in cyberspace".

The international community has been actively involved for more than twenty years[35] in the effort of identifying agreed rules

---

[33] "Superiority through persistence seizes and maintains the initiative in cyberspace by continuously engaging and contesting adversaries and causing them uncertainty wherever they maneuver. It describes *how* we operate – maneuvering seamlessly between defence and offense across the interconnected battlespace. It describes *where* we operate – globally, as close as possible to adversaries and their operations. It describes *when* we operate – continuously, shaping the battlespace. It describes *why* we operate – to create operational advantage for us while denying the same to our adversaries", Ibid., p. 6.

[34] J. Healey, "Triggering the New Forever War, in Cyberspace", The Cipher Brief, 1 April 2018.

[35] "Back in 1998 (while Operation "Moonlight Maze", one of the first and most devastating cyber campaign ever orchestrated by Russia's intelligence against US military targets, was well underway...) the Russian Federation presented to the UN General Assembly a proposal for a Resolution titled "Developments in the field of information and telecommunications in the context of international security". The Russians wanted to discuss both cyber security and the limitations to destabilising online content (revealingly gathered together by Moscow under the label of "threats to the information space"). The West refused to have that discussion, on the ground, essentially, of its self-proclaimed moral superiority: if we want to safeguard an open Internet and freedom of expression, the West argued, it is not possible to negotiate about information's content. Ironically, almost twenty years later, the West is forced to discuss with Moscow about the threat of manipulated online content, which probably is, in itself, a score on the Russian side". F. Rugge, *Mind Hacking: Information Warfare in the Cyber Age*, ISPI Analysis no. 319, January 2018, pp. 3-4, reproduced by the *Global Solutions Journal*,

of states' behaviour in cyberspace, but little has been accomplished. If a cyber armaments' control regime seems unlikely to emerge in the next future, as trust among key international players is low and verification of compliancy is impossible, some encouraging progress has been achieved so far within OSCE. Two sets of confidence building measures (CBMs) have been so far adopted, listing (indeed very general) voluntary commitments of the member-states to "establish international level of expectations about states' behaviour in cyberspace"[36] with the purpose to improve stability and encourage trust, cooperation and transparency among states. Together with other international efforts devoted to specify constraining norms of international law applicable to the conduct of states in cyberspace (especially with the work of the Group of Governmental Experts within the United Nations, and the two Tallinn Manuals elaborated by the NATO Cooperative Cyber Defence Center of Excellence), these measures help enhance predictability – and, therefore, provide some order - within the international community by establishing what is the prevalent *opinio juris* about permissible behaviour in cyberspace, and by ensuring channels of communication that might one day prove useful to mitigate and defuse crisis stemming from the ongoing international confrontation. However, they certainly do not constitute enforceable norms of conduct[37].

---

vol. 1, no. 1, May 2018.

[36] P. Pawlak, "Confidence-Building Measures in Cyberspace: Current Debates and Trends", in A.-M. Osula and H. Rõigas (eds.) *International Cyber Norms: Legal Policy and Industry Perspectives*, NATO CCD COE Publications, Tallinn, 2016 pp. 129-53.

[37] "At this stage, large scale formal treaties regulating cyber space seem unlikely. Over the past decade, the UN General Assembly has passed a series of resolutions condemning criminal activity and drawing attention to defensive measures that governments can take. For more than a decade, Russia has sought a treaty for broader international oversight of the Internet, banning deception or the embedding of malicious code or circuitry that could be activated in the event of war. But Americans have argued that measures banning offense can damage defence against current attacks, and would be impossible to verify or enforce. Moreover,

In this environment of uncertainty, it is therefore no surprise if the most noteworthy successes in international cooperation have been achieved within long-standing political and military alliances and regional organisations, where values, interests and trust that bind states together allow firm steps even in unchartered domains. This is recognised also in the new National Cyber Strategy of the US, with which the United States also launches a "Cyber Deterrence Initiative" that aims at strengthening internationally coordinated responses to cyber attacks in order to "send a stronger message", so that "the adversaries understand the consequences of malicious cyber behaviour"[38]. This initiative is directly connected to the US efforts in international cyber capacity-building, so that allies can contribute to the US-led international coalition overall capability of attributing cyber attacks, establishing deterrence, and promoting the emergence of international norms of state behaviour in cyberspace[39].

---

the United States has resisted agreements that could legitimise authoritarian governments' censorship of the Internet. Nonetheless, the United States has begun informal discussions with Russia. Even advocates for an international law for information operations are skeptical of a multilateral treaty akin to the Geneva Conventions that could contain precise and detailed rules given future technological volatility, but they argue that like minded states could announce self governing rules that could form norms for the future", J.S. Nye Jr (2010), p. 18.

[38] "The United States will formalise and make routine how we work with like-minded partners to attribute and deter malicious cyber activities with integrated strategies that impose swift, costly, and transparent consequences when malicious actors harm the United States or our partners. […] The imposition of consequences will be more impactful and send a stronger message if it is carried out in concert with a broader coalition of like-minded states. The United States will launch an international Cyber Deterrence Initiative to build such a coalition and develop tailored strategies to ensure adversaries understand the consequences of their malicious cyber behaviour. The United States will work with like-minded states to coordinate and support each other's responses to significant malicious cyber incidents, including through intelligence sharing, buttressing of attribution claims, public statements of support for responsive actions taken, and joint imposition of consequences against malign actors", National Security Strategy of the United States of America…, cit., p. 21.

[39] "Our leadership in building partner cybersecurity capacity is critical to

Participating in the US-led Cyber Deterrence Initiative coalition would not only mean sharing the values and the objectives set forth by the US National Cyber Strategy, but it would also be fully coherent with the so-called "EU cyber diplomatic toolbox" that was adopted by the EU in September 2017 to coordinate member states' responses to malicious cyber activities[40]. Moreover, being a functional member of this alliance represents an excellent opportunity for strengthening, at the operational level, situational awareness' and attribution's capabilities, reinforcing our law enforcement's efforts, magnifying our diplomatic undertakings, facilitating information and intelligence sharing. At the national level, it represents a powerful incentive to promote, *inter alia*, appropriate investments in cyber capabilities and to streamline of our decision-making processes for responding to cyber crisis. In any case, in a context characterised by an intrinsic asymmetry such as the cyber domain, the best possible strategy of defence would be that of partnering at all levels with those that are defending against the same menace.

In order to face these challenges, counter these risks and advance its vision of cyberspace the US National Cyber Strategy

---

maintaining American influence against global competitors. Building partner cyber capacity will empower international partners to implement policies and practices which allow them to be effective partners in the United States-led Cyber Deterrence Initiative", Ibid., p. 26.

[40] "The recently adopted framework for a joint EU diplomatic response to malicious cyber activities (the "cyber diplomacy toolbox") sets out the measures under the Common Foreign and Security Policy, including restrictive measures which can be used to strengthen the EU's response to activities that harm its political, security and economic interests. The framework constitutes an important step in the development of signaling and reactive capacities at EU and Member State level. It will increase our capacity to attribute malicious cyber activities, with the aim of influencing the behaviour of potential aggressors, while taking into account the need to ensure proportionate responses", "Joint Communication to the European Parliament and the Council. Resilience, Deterrence and Defence: Building strong cybersecurity for the EU", Brussels, 13 September 2017, JOIN(2017) 450 final, p. 16. The "toolbox" is available at http://www.consilium.europa.eu/en/press/press-releases/2017/06/19-cyber-diplomacy-toolbox/

envisages a wide-ranging initiative to actively promote (enforce?) at the global level an open, uncensored, interoperable, reliable and secure Internet connectivity[41]. The link between Internet freedom and the US national interest it clearly explained in the National Cyber Strategy, when is stated that "[T]he United States will continue to work with like-minded countries, industry, civil society, and other stakeholders to advance human rights and Internet freedom globally and to counter authoritarian efforts to censor and influence Internet development"[42].

We will see whether, in the long run, the US efforts to promote a global and uncensored Internet connectivity will be coroneted by success, to the benefit of individual freedoms globally – although not necessarily in favour of international stability. At first sight, and notwithstanding "the enduring attraction of free and open societies" on international public opinions[43], in-

---

[41] "The United States will continue to lead by example and push back against unjustifiable barriers to the free flow of data and digital trade", National Cyber Strategy of the United States of America…, cit., p. 24.
Commenting the new National Cyber Strategy, Christopher Painter, Commissioner on the Global Commission for the Stability of Cyberspace and formerly the top cyber diplomat at the US Department of State wrote: "But, there's a lot to like in this strategy even if it lacks real detail and often resorts to vague platitudes. It restates much of the US cyber canon, including the importance of Internet freedom and the central role of multi stakeholder Internet governance, welcome pronouncements to our allies and partners. That's even more important now when attacks on the press and claims of 'fake news' often dominate the headlines and call into question our commitment to these ideals and when countries including China and Russia advance a contrary agenda of absolute Internet sovereignty", C. Painter (2018).

[42] The United States Government will continue to support civil society through integrated support for technology development, digital safety training, policy advocacy, and research. These programs aim to enhance the ability of individual citizens, activists, human rights defenders, independent journalists, civil society organisations, and marginalised populations to safely access the uncensored Internet and promote Internet freedom at the local, regional, national, and international levels.

[43] Last November, at the traditional Lord Mayor's Banquet, Great Britain's Prime Minister, Theresa May, referred to Russia's influence campaign, and warned: "So

ternational law and the principle of sovereignty appear to play in favour of those states controlling Internet content and the connectivity available to their citizens.

## Sovereignity and the Nature of Cyberspace

The cyber domain has proved to be too relevant for national security not to become, also, the arena where national interests naturally collide. If, in the words of the latest National Security Strategy of the United States, "sovereign states are the best hope for a peaceful world"[44], it is around the principle of sovereignty – and through available political-military alliances – that we will have to find the means to enforce order in the cyber domain[45], while preserving the Internet as a "global common" available both to international society and humankind. If, on the one hand, states are certainly among the most relevant and accountable actors of international security (even if, as we have seen, this is not necessarily always the case in cyberspace), on the other, at least from the analytical point of view, it remains to be seen whether the Westfalian society of territorial sovereign states is the most suitable principle to provide order and stability to the complexity brought by the digital revolution.

---

I have a very simple message for Russia. We know what you are doing. And you will not succeed. Because you underestimate the resilience of our democracies, the enduring attraction of free and open societies, and the commitment of Western nations to the alliances that bind us".

[44] "This strategy is guided by principled realism. It is realist because it acknowledges the central role of power in international politics, affirms that sovereign states are the best hope for a peaceful world, and clearly defines our national interests. It is principled because it is grounded in the knowledge that advancing American principles spreads peace and prosperity around the globe. We are guided by our values and disciplined by our interests", National Security Strategy of the United States of America…, cit., p. 55.

[45] "Providing security is a classic function of government, and some observers believe that increasing insecurity will lead to an increased role for governments in cyberspace. Many states desire to extend their sovereignty in cyberspace, and seek technological means to do so", J.S. Nye Jr (2010), p. 15.

Cyberspace is for the greatest part privately owned and operated, it is borderless, it has become an essential platform for most of contemporary endeavours, and it is the layer upon which individuals create billions of connections across geographical borders, sharing knowledge and redesigning the world at an unprecedented speed. The cyber domain is home to non-state actors (Internet providers, search engines, social media, formal and informal communities, etc.) whose influence over the Internet is comparable to – or greater of – that of many sovereign states. Cyberspace has become, and will most likely increasingly be, an environment characterised by an "unthinkable complexity"[46], where a multitude of diverse players constantly connect throughout the globe generating "an inescapable network of mutuality"[47]. As such, scholars will have to investigate whether the cause of order in the cyber domain might be served more appropriately by – and better understood, from the analytical point of view, with – a not state-centric approach[48]. The

[46] William Gibson, in *Neuromancer*, uses in 1984 for the first time the term "cyberspace", and defines it as follow: "Cyberspace. A *consensual hallucination* experienced daily by billions of legitimate operators, in every nation, by children being taught mathematical concepts. [...] A graphic representation of data abstracted from the banks of every computer in the human system. *Unthinkable complexity*. Lines of light ranged in the nonspace of the mind, clusters and constellations of data. Like city lights, receding" (italic mine).

[47] In a speech delivered in Alabama in 1963, Martin Luther King affirmed "Injustice anywhere is a threat to justice everywhere. We are caught in an inescapable network of mutuality, tied in a single garment of destiny. Whatever affects one directly, affects all indirectly." I believe that this statement, which embodies the highest moral authority of the US civil rights' movement, perfectly describes one of the most critical challenge of our generation: that of ensuring a secure and just order in cyberspace.

[48] L. Kello, "The Meaning of the Cyber Revolution: Perils to Theory and Statecraft", *International Security*, vol. 38, no. 2, Fall 2013, p. 38: "Within the field of international security studies, conceptions of system and order typically – and at times exclusively – center on states and competition among them. To be sure, this frame applies to much of the cyber issue; insofar as it does not, however, future study will require consideration of the negative influences that nonstate players may be able to exert on states and their relations with other states. Cyber studies require a willingness to evaluate the cyber issue in its interstate as well

example of the original development of the Internet, and the governance structure currently sustaining its everyday functioning, are both good examples of how, in abstract, states are *not necessary* to create and sustain cyberspace – they are in fact, to a certain extent, "special guests" of cyberspace[49]. The governance of the Internet Corporation for Assigned Names and Numbers (ICANN), whose mission is to help ensure a stable, secure and unified global Internet, is a tangible proof of how a multi-stakeholders regime, where states sit together with private companies and many other different participants, may, in fact, be the most suitable arrangement for allowing order to emerge from within the complexity of the Internet.

The International Society was established in Westphalia on the idea that the monopoly of force within the territory of the state was also the "ticket" necessary for accessing the "club of sovereign states", that are *per se sufficientes*, equals among them and *superiorem non recognoscentes*[50]. This "external dimension of sovereignty" was the intellectual construct that allowed the newly formed "club" of sovereign states to shape many formal and informal[51] "institutions" in order to ensure an acceptable level of order within the anarchy that was emerging on the ashes

---

as in its global dimensions – especially the points at which the two universes converge and collide".

[49] "Governments of the Industrial World, you weary giants of flesh and steel, I come from Cyberspace, the new home of Mind. On behalf of the future, I ask you of the past to leave us alone. You are not welcome among us. You have no sovereignty where we gather. We have no elected government, nor are we likely to have one, so I address you with no greater authority than that with which liberty itself always speaks. I declare the global social space we are building to be naturally independent of the tyrannies you seek to impose on us. You have no moral right to rule us nor do you possess any methods of enforcement we have true reason to fear", J.P. Barlow (1996).

[50] C.A.W. Manning, *The Nature of International Society*, London and Basingstoke, MacMillan Education, 1975.

[51] "By an institution we do not necessarily imply an organisation or administrative machinery, but rather a set of habits and practices shaped toward the realisation of common goals", H. Bull, "The Anarchical Society. A Study of Order in World Politics", Basingstoke, Palgrave, 1977, p. 74.

of the medieval *Respublica Christiana*: communication (diplomacy), the definition of what is acceptable behaviour in the absence of a higher-ranking authority (international law), the most rudimental operating principles (the role of great powers), the protection of its very existence (the Balance of Power)[52]. At the basis of the emergence of these essential "building blocks" of the international community there was Grotius' genius, who conceived the idea of a self-sustaining society of sovereign states regulated by "natural law" and by a peculiar set of principles and norms valid only among themselves, and that allowed a pragmatic tolerance of diversity within an overall structure of values[53]. This was the hypostatic abstraction that laid the ground for the International Society as we know it[54].

Maybe it is by following Grotius steps and by looking at cyberspace as an hypostatic abstraction of its own, with its own peculiar functioning norms and principles and with a set of authorities that include sovereign states along with many others, that it would be possible to overcome the limits intrinsic in a purely state-centric approach in cyberspace. What appears to be certain is that enforcing an order that does not reflect the complexity of cyberspace will be more and more difficult, especially given the speed of the technological revolution underway. We might live in times in which politics seem unable to determine our path into the future, but we may look in the distance by sitting on the shoulders of the giants. And we certainly need all the help we can get.

---

[52] Ibid., Part 2, pp. 95-221.

[53] Being states "cognitively equal, in possession of the same equipment for interpreting the world", these institutions were not "an attempt to provide a solution to a moral problem, but [as] a way of acknowledging its existence", J. Mayall, "International Society and International theory", in M. Donelan (ed.), *The Reason of States. A study in International Political Theory*, London, Routledge, 1978, p. 127.

[54] "A society of states (or international society) exists when a group of states, conscious of certain common interests and common values, form a society in the sense that they conceive themselves to be bound by a common set of rules in their relations with one another, and share in the working of common institutions", H. Bull (1977), p. 13.

# 2. Russia: Information Security Meets Cyber Security[1]

Tim Maurer, Garrett Hinck

In 2009, Timothy Thomas, a Russia expert at the Foreign Military Studies Office at Ford Leavensforth in the US warned that, "[p]erhaps more than any other country, Russia is alarmed over the cognitive aspects of cyber issues as much as their technical aspects". This warning, delivered seven years before the hack of the Democratic National Committee in the United States, highlights that Moscow has taken a different, a more comprehensive and integrated approach to information security compared to Western capitals' focus on more technical network-centric cyber security. Outlined explicitly in doctrines and strategies over the past two decades, it is becoming increasingly clear how Russia is implementing this perspective in practice – quite successfully so far one may add.

Analysts of Russian policy emphasise that the Russian government has been primarily concerned about internal stability and external efforts to undermine it[2]. "[Russian b]ooks and articles claim that "the death blow to the Soviet Union came, not from

[1] Parts of this are based and include *extracts* from Cyber Mercenaries: The State, Hackers, and Power by Tim Maurer. © Tim Maurer 2018, published by Cambridge University Press, reproduced with permission.

[2] N. Inkster, *China's Cyber Power*, New York, Routledge, 2016, p. 124; T. Thomas, "Comparing Chinese and Russian Cyber Concepts", in T. Thomas (ed.), *Three Faces of the Cyber Dragon: Cyber Peace Activist, Spook, Attacker*, Fort Leavenworth, KS, Foreign Military Studies Office, 2012.

NATO conventional forces, but from an imperialist 'information war' that Russia lost," according to Thomas, explaining why "By 2000, therefore, Russian state specialists had written the country's first information security doctrine (perhaps the first of any nation in the world)"[3]. This historic narrative of what led to the fall of the Soviet Union partly explains Russia's current efforts to control information and the Internet in Russia. It is therefore no surprise that Russia's Information Security Doctrine of 2000 focused not only on the external but also on the internal threat dimension, defining information security as "protection of [Russia's] national interests in the information sphere defined by the totality of balanced interests of the individual, society, and the state"[4].

Internationally, Russia's diplomatic initiatives reflect both domestic concerns over the free flow of information and the military's approach toward information operations and cybersecurity. In the mid-1990s, the Kremlin approached the White House with a proposal for an international information security treaty. Although the US government rejected the proposal, this has not kept the Russian government from pursuing and promoting the idea globally. Moscow put the implications of information and communications technologies for international peace and security on the agenda of the UN General Assembly's First Committee in the late 1990s and worked with the member states of the Shanghai Cooperation Organization (SCO) to further advance its proposal for such a treaty. Together with China, Russia developed the aforementioned 2011 draft International Code of Conduct for Information Security, along with a draft Convention that circulated at a conference in Yekaterinburg in the fall of 2011. Remarks given by Sergei Smirnov, the first Deputy Director of the Federal Security Service (FSB), at a meeting of the SCO revealed the motivation behind these efforts: "New technologies [are being] used by Western special

[3] T. Thomas, "Nation-state Cyber Strategies: Examples from China and Russia", in F.D. Kramer, S.H. Starr, and L.K. Wentz (eds.), *Cyber Power and National Security*, National Defense University Press, Potomac Books, 2009, p. 486.
[4] Ibid., pp. 481-82.

services to create and maintain a level of continual tension in society, with serious intentions extending even to regime change [...] Our elections, especially the [2012] presidential election and the situation in the preceding period, revealed the potential of the blogosphere"[5].

The Russian perception that information constitutes a threat dates back to the Bolsheviks. As Andrei Soldatov and Irina Borogan, two Russian investigative journalists, have pointed out, "The Bolsheviks wanted newspapers to organise and mobilise the masses, not to inform them"[6]. The Communist Party therefore focused on establishing an effective censorship regime partly based on using intimidation to encourage self-censorship. There is evidence that President Putin has similarly been concerned about Russia's political stability since his days as Yeltsin's Protégé and Director of the FSB in the late 1990s[7]. Putin's ascent to power coincided with the Russian government's push to strengthen its control over the media following the demise of the Soviet Union. Soldatov and Borogan have traced how over the years, the government worked with friendly oligarchs to buy media companies and Internet platforms and control them through ownership[8]. These renewed efforts to increase the state's control over information coincided with the establishment of pro-Kremlin youth organisations, partly as a counterbalance to potential popular uprisings[9]. This concern over domestic stability also affected the bureaucratic structure of the state itself. For example, in the wake of global financial crisis of 2007-2008, Dmitry Medvedev, President of the Russian Federation at the time, created a new Interior Ministry department that focused, together with the FSB, on monitoring for early signs of popular unrest[10].

---

[5] A. Soldatov and I. Borogan, *The Red Web: The Struggle Between Russia's Digital Dictators and the New Online Revolutionaries*, New York, Public Affairs, 2015, p. 163.

[6] Ibid., p. 11.

[7] Ibid., pp. 88-89.

[8] Ibid., p. 109.

[9] Ibid., p. 113.

[10] Ibid., pp. 113-15.

The Colour Revolutions in Georgia and Ukraine and the Arab Spring of 2011 fuelled the Kremlin's perception of threat. As Soldatov and Borogan pointed out, "It was not lost on Putin and his people that the events in Tunisia and Egypt were widely characterised as Facebook and Twitter revolutions. Putin and his entourage became worried that this time the United States had found a truly magic tool that could bring people to the streets without any organising structure: the Internet"[11]. In response, the Russian government started to further tighten its control on the Internet. In addition to DDoS (distributed denial of service) attacks against blogging platforms[12], an increasing number of technical controls were put in place. In July 2012, a new law was signed allowing the government to filter content on the Internet[13]. The law also used a narrative of sovereign democracy and digital sovereignty to pressure companies like Google and Facebook to store data on Russian territory. Placing servers within Russia's borders would enable the government to gain access to the data via the SORM (literally "System for Operative Investigative Activities") black boxes that were already running on Russia's telecommunications infrastructure and allowing the government to surveil communications[14].

The 2014 ouster of Ukrainian president Yanukovych struck even closer to home than the Arab Spring[15]. In response, a April 2014 decree led to the combination of the existing SORM-based surveillance system with deep packet inspection, and added a legal requirement that servers be located on Russian territory. A new Russian information security doctrine adopted in 2015, the first since 2000, articulated the heightened sense of threat, stating that "[t]he special services of certain states

[11] Ibid., pp. 124-25.

[12] Ibid., p. 149.

[13] Ibid., pp. 166-67.

[14] V. Shtepa, "Russia's Draft Information Security Doctrine at Odds with Realities of Modern Information Environment", *Eurasia Daily Monitor*, vol. 13, no. 128, 2016.

[15] A. Soldatov and I. Borogan (2015), pp. 259-60.

provide information and psychological influence, aimed at destabilising the political and social situation in various regions of the world, resulting in the undermining of the sovereignty and the territorial integrity of other states"[16]. Even so, Soldatov and Borogan pointed out, the Russian government's efforts to control information are much subtler than in other countries. Actual arrests of journalists or raids by the police are rare; according to Soldatov and Borogan, "The Putin approach is all about intimidation, more often than actual coercion, as an instrument of control"[17].

When it comes to the Russian military, the same focus on information shines through. The 2010 Military Doctrine of the Russian Federation, for example, described information warfare as an instrument "to achieve political objectives without the utilisation of military force" and in combination with conventional means as a tool to create "a favourable response from the world community"[18]. In 2011, the Russian Ministry of Defense also published Conceptual Views on the Activities of the Armed Forces of the Russian Federation in Information Space. This document defines information war as

> [c]onflict between two or more States in information space with the goal of inflicting damage to information systems, processes, and resources, as well as to critically important structures and other structures; undermining political, economic, and social systems; carrying out mass psychological campaigns against the population of a State in order to destabilise society and the government; as well as forcing a State to make decisions in the interests of their opponents[19].

---

[16] V. Shtepa (2016).

[17] A. Soldatov and I. Borogan (2015), pp. 313-14.

[18] A. Segal, *The Hacked World Order: How Nations Fight, Trade, Maneuver, and Manipulate in the Digital Age*, New York, Public Affairs, 2016, p. 70.

[19] T. Thomas, *Russian Military Strategy: Impacting 21st Century Reform and Geopolitics*, Fort Leavenworth, KS, Foreign Military Studies Office, 2015, p. 281.

The following year, Deputy Prime Minister Dmitry Rogozin announced the establishment of a new branch in the Russian military and creation of a cyber command[20].

A shift in Russian thinking apparently occurred in 2013 that moved them even further away from a focus on cyber attacks on infrastructure and towards information operations. That year, Valery Gerasimov, Chief of the General Staff of the Russian Armed Forces, published his influential essay that outlined what's been coined "hybrid warfare". In the words of Pavel Zolotarev, a retired Russian general, "we had come to the conclusion, having analysed the actions of Western countries in the post-Soviet space – first of all the United States – that manipulation in the information sphere is a very effective tool". The Internet had provided a new set of tools that could replace what Zolotarev called "grandfather-style methods: scatter leaflets, throw around some printed materials, manipulate the radio or television"[21]. The Ukrainians have experienced the full force of this new strategy. Ever more details are being documented about the Kremlin's army of trolls that is paid to confuse, disinform, and subvert its target audiences. Reports suggest that this approach was expanded in the fall of 2013 and driven by Vyacheslav Volodin, the deputy chief of the presidential administration in Moscow[22]. The trolls number in the hundreds, work in twelve-hour shifts and are required to post 135 comments a day on online message boards and media websites[23]. They are part of a broader network of proxies the Russian government has been using to project soft power in its pursuit to retain regime hegemony[24].

---

[20] A. Segal (2016), p. 93.

[21] E. Osnos, D. Remnick, and J. Yaffa, "Trump, Putin, and the New Cold War", *The New Yorker*, 6 March 2017.

[22] A. Soldatov and I. Borogan (2015), p. 282.

[23] Ibid., p. 284.

[24] O. Lutsevych, *Agents of the Russian World: Proxy Groups in the Contested Neighbourhood*, London, Chatham House, 2016, p. 2.

In other words, this solidification in the Russian government's views on information security and the use of information operations is reflected in its actual behaviour. While it stands accused of causing a power outage in Western Ukraine with a cyber attack, such disruptive events have been rare. Instead, Russia is more focused on using information operations to achieve its political goals.

## A Particular Phenomenon in Russia: The Nexus Between the State and Criminals

Former Soviet states stand out for their many individuals with highly developed technical skills and their university departments in math, engineering, and computer science, which have ranked among the world's best for decades. It is the result of systematic literacy campaigns after the 1917 revolution, with the campaigns boosting the literacy rate from 22% at the beginning of the twentieth century to full literacy by the time the Soviet Union collapsed. While states that used to be part of the Soviet Union still rank among the world's most literate and educated societies, unemployment has risen and the economy has not been able to absorb this technically skilled workforce[25]. The economic crash in 1998 exacerbated the problem, with only an estimated 50% of Russian software companies surviving the downturn and a concomitant rise in cyber crime[26]. The same challenges persist today. In sum, there is no labour shortage in the region when it comes to information technology and hacking, but the legitimate industry is not big enough to absorb all of the labour and government salaries of a few thousand dollars a year pale in comparison to reports of thousands or millions made in the latest cyber heist.

---

[25] B.N. Mironov, "The Development of Literacy in Russia and the USSR from the Tenth to the Twentieth Centuries", *History of Education Quarterly*, vol. 31, no. 2, 1991.

[26] R. Alvey, "Russian hackers for hire: the rise of the emercenary", *Janes Intelligence Review*, vol. 1, no. 7, 2001, pp. 52-53.

At the turn of the century, several hundred Russians had already participated in hacking competitions such as the one organised by www.hackzone.ru and hacker magazines had a monthly circulation in the tens of thousands[27]. A decade later the Moscow-based cybersecurity company Group-IB estimated the size of the cyber crime market in Russia alone to be US$2.3 billion[28]. Since hackers take great care not to target people within the area of the former Soviet Union but focus on victims in the United States and Europe, it is not surprising that few arrests are made by Russian law enforcement agencies[29]. The latter often do not respond to requests for assistance from foreign law enforcement agencies and frequently protest when Russian nationals are arrested abroad[30]. For example, when Vladimir Drinkman was arrested while vacationing in Amsterdam in 2012, the Russian government tried to block the US government's extradition request by filing its own extradition request, thereby at least delaying prosecution[31].

The cyber crime expert Misha Glenny has expressed doubts that Russian law enforcement is weak and the government unable to take action. He argued that "Russian law enforcement and the FSB in particular have a very good idea of what is going on and they are monitoring it but as long as the fraud is restricted to other parts of the world they don't care"[32]. The FSB's role is particularly important given its management of the SORM monitoring system, and as Thomas has documented, the FSB law has been amended to allow it "to conduct police investigations to counter

---

[27] Ibid., pp. 52-53.

[28] A. de Carbonnel, "Hackers for hire: Ex-Soviet tech geeks play outsized role in global cyber crime", *NBC News*, 22 August 2013.

[29] N. Perlroth, "After Arrest of Accused Hacker, Russia Accuses U.S. of Kidnapping", Bits (blog), *The New York Times*, 8 July 2014.

[30] B. Krebs, "Story-Driven Résumé: My Best Work 2005-2009", Krebs on Security (blog), 29 December 2009.

[31] M. Goldstein and N. Perlroth, "Authorities Closing In on Hackers Who Stole Data From JPMorgan Chase", Dealbook, *The New York Times*, 15 March 2015.

[32] A. de Carbonnel (2013).

threats to Russia's information security"[33]. Another indication that the Russian government can effectively enforce the law if it so chooses is the fact that malware used by Russian and East European cyber criminals is often designed so that it "purposefully avoids infecting computers if the program detects the potential victim is a native resident"[34]. For example, "installscash.com" pays people money for installing their adware and spyware on machines in dozens of countries but points out on its website that "[w]e do not purchase Russian and CIS traffic". (When Russian hackers do target victims in Russia, the Moscow's response is swift and harsh. In 2012, eight men were arrested by Russian police after stealing some US$4 million from several dozen banks, including some in Russia. According to Krebs, "Russian police released a video showing one of the suspects loudly weeping in the moments following a morning raid on his home"[35]).

Tolerating such criminal activity can turn into more proactive interest from the government. In some cases, working with the government helps avoid arrest, as described by Oleg Gordievsky, the former head of the KGB office in London, who said in 1998 that "[t]here are organised groups of hackers tied to the FSB and pro-Chechen sites have been hacked into by such groups [...] One man I know, who was caught committing a cyber crime, was given the choice of either prison or cooperation with the FSB and he went along"[36]. In such cases, in return for their cooperation, the hackers not only avoid prison, but are actively defended by the Russian government. Alexander Klimburg and Heli Tirmaa-Klaar described one such case from 2004, in which the Tomsk FSB office described malicious activity against pro-Chechen websites as being legal and "simply an 'expression of [the hackers'] political position, which is worthy of respect'". This system of the FSB turning hackers into

[33] T. Thomas (2015), p. 267.

[34] B. Krebs (2009).

[35] B. Krebs, "A Busy Week for Cyber Crime Justice", Krebs on Security (blog), 26 March 2012.

[36] R. Alvey (2001), pp. 52-53.

proxies for internal and external offensive cyber operations was also reaffirmed by Sergei Pokrovsky, the editor of the hacking magazine *Khaker*, and Vasilyev, a convicted hacker and the head of the Moscow Civil Hacking School[37].

## Known Cyber Campaigns: A Selection

Much has been written about the malicious cyber activity targeting Estonia in 2007, Georgia in 2008, and Ukraine since 2014. Yet, the most detailed account describing Russian cyber campaigns are several indictments that the US Department of Justice unsealed starting in 2017. These indictments offer unparalleled insight into how Russia applies its view of information security to pursue its political goals and how it engages with hackers that are not part of Russia's military or intelligence agencies. The following three indictments discussed in greater detail serve as case studies illustrating how the Russia states wields its power in cyberspace by using and sometimes combining offensive cyber operations and information operations.

First, in early 2017, the US Department of Justice charged two hackers and two FSB officers for hacking Yahoo. This indictment brought to light how Russia uses cyber criminals to aid its hacking efforts and how it uses hacking to pursue its political ends. A year later, Special Counsel Robert Mueller indicted the Internet Research Agency and thirteen of its employees for their efforts to influence the 2016 US election using social media. The Internet Research Agency's activities are a perfect example in practice of how Russia's view of "information security" extends to a much broader set of areas than the Western "cybersecurity" concept. Third, in July 2018, the US Department of Justice indicted twelve hackers from the Russian military intelligence service for their involvement in the hack of the Democratic National Committee (DNC) and publication of Clinton campaign documents.

---

[37] Ibid.

## Case study #1: the Yahoo hack

The Yahoo hack was the biggest data breach of all time highlighting Russia's deliberate use of offensive cyber operations. Its massive set of user data would have been an incentive to any cyber criminal. But in its March 2017 indictment, the Justice Department alleged that two Russian FSB officers and two cyber criminals hacked Yahoo not for financial purposes but for political espionage. Details in the indictment revealed the surprising finding that the compromise of one of the world's largest email providers was primarily for intelligence gathering purposes. As a case study, the Yahoo hack indictment also reveals the depth of the relationship between Russian security services and cyber criminals The two FSB officers, Igor Anatolyevich Sushchin and Dmitry Aleksandrovich Dokuchaev, both members of the FSB's Center for Information Security, masterminded a plot to use two hackers, Karim Baratov and Alexsey Alexseyevich Belan, to compromise Yahoo's networks and email accounts associated with targets of value to Russia intelligence[38]. Their scheme ran from January 2014 to December 2016.

The indictment shows that the Yahoo hack was about internal security as much as foreign espionage. A large proportion of the identified targets had to do with dissidents, Russian companies and even officials within the Russian government. Targeting these individuals through Yahoo had geopolitical implications: the FSB had to compromise a massive American company (and in the process cost it hundreds of millions) in order to spy on Russians and their neighbours.

On a basic level, Suschin and Dokuchaev's plot was simple. Instead of breaking into their intelligence targets' emails one-by-one, they would break into Yahoo and kill thousands of birds with one hack. But they needed help from cyber criminals to break into Yahoo's complex network. Meanwhile, Alexsey

---

[38] "U.S. Charges Russian FSB Officers and Their Criminal Conspirators for Hacking Yahoo and Millions of Email Accounts", Department of Justice press release, 15 March 2017.

Belan had returned to Russia at the perfect time. By 2013 the Department of Justice had already indicted him twice for thefts of user data from US e-commerce companies. He narrowly escaped extradition to the US by fleeing to his homeland that year. It was up to the Russian government whether to hand over Belan pursuant to an Interpol Red Notice. As the indictment alleged, "Rather than arrest him, the FSB officers used him"[39]. Dokuchaev and Suschin put Belan to work compromising Yahoo's network and then targeting specific persons of interest. The FSB's refusal to cooperate with Western law enforcement is indicative of the Russian government's approach of turn-by-turn toleration and outright enlistment of cyber criminals[40].

At Dokuchaev and Suschin's direction, Belan broke into Yahoo's network and stole a backup copy of Yahoo's user database. This theft enabled the team to access individual targeted email accounts by counterfeiting authentication information associated with the accounts[41]. Among their targets: Russian journalists and politicians who criticised the Kremlin, former officials from Russia's neighbours, US government officials, and officers at US technology companies[42]. Belan's efforts had pointed out that some of the targets had non-Yahoo email accounts through providers like Google. This is where Karim Baratov came into the picture. Baratov was a Canadian national living in Canada who advertised his services on Russian "hacker-for-hire" forums. Dokuchaev paid him, about $US100 per account, to compromise emails of interest to the FSB that were from non-Yahoo providers[43].

---

[39] Indictment at 2, *United States v. Dokuchaev et al.*, No. 17-CR-00103 N.D. Ca. filed 28 February 2017.

[40] See for a fuller view on these relationships: T. Maurer, *Cyber Mercenaries: The State, Hackers, and Power,* Cambridge, Cambridge University Press, 2018, pp. 103-106.

[41] Indictment at 7-8, *United States v. Dokuchaev et al....*, cit.

[42] Ibid., 10-11.

[43] "Canadian Hacker Who Conspired With and Aided Russian FSB Officers Pleads Guilty", Department of Justice press release, 28 November 2017.

The Justice Department's documentation of these targets suggests that the FSB carried out the hack for domestic purposes as well as international espionage. In April 2015, Suschin order Dokuchaev to target senior officers at a Russian financial company and later referred to that company as "the main target"[44]. Other internal targets included an assistant to the deputy chairman of the Russian federation, an officer at the Russian Ministry of Internal Affairs, and officers at a major Russian cybersecurity firm[45]. Some of these targets could have been the FSB's internal rivals, and others could have been potential targets because they politically opposed the Putin regime. However, prioritising internal political spying is consistent with the FSB's domestic security portfolio[46]. While the Yahoo hack may have yielded rich intelligence gains to the FSB, it had devastating economic consequences for Yahoo. News of the breach, which exposed 500 million users' data to the FSB, caused a US$350 million reduction in Yahoo's sale price to Verizon in February 2017[47].

## Case study #2: the Internet Research Agency

The Internet Research Agency's social media influence campaign is a vivid example of how Western governments failed to grasp the implications of Russia's approach toward information security. The small organisation of "professional trolls" in St. Petersburg demonstrated that by manipulating social media platforms they could fan the flames of partisanship and worsen US political divisions. As described in the Justice Department's February 2018 indictment, the Internet Research Agency (IRA) conducted a multi-year campaign of "information warfare

---

[44] Ibid., pp. 12 and 16.

[45] Ibid., p. 14.

[46] For a recent article, see A. Soldatov, "Putin's Secret Services: How the Kremlin Corralled the FSB", *Foreign Affairs*, 31 May 2018.

[47] S. Fiegerman, "Verizon cuts Yahoo deal price by $350 million", *CNN*, 21 February 2017.

against the United States of America"[48]. The "translator project" that focused on US social media outlets like YouTube, Facebook, Instagram, and Twitter started in April 2014 and conducted operations against US social media through February 2018[49]. The information warfare strategy intensified partisan rhetoric and circulated false and hyperbolic narratives that exacerbated distrust of the US political establishment.

No US intelligence agencies or defence officials had publicly warned about influence operations over social media prior to the 2016 election. Cybersecurity analysts failed to grasp the threat to democratic politics from foreign actors on social media. In contrast, the Russian government had long warned about the dangers of "information operations". The IRA campaign was a move to wield information as a weapon against the US domestic population, following on the heels of trial runs in Ukraine and other former Soviet republics[50]. What's remarkable about the IRA is that it shows how Russia shifted from fearing information operations against its own population to using them against its opponents.

As the Department of Justice wrote, the IRA "had a strategic goal to sow discord in the US political system"[51]. The consistent theme in IRA-produced content is a distrust of establishment politicians, symbolised in Hillary Clinton. By weaponising social media tools, including advertisements, the IRA was able to spread that message to hundreds of thousands of social media users in the US IRA employees accomplished this goal by setting up pages that posed as authentic US political groups – "Secured Borders," "Blactivist", and "Army of Jesus", on social media platforms like Facebook[52]. But it was all fraud. IRA workers faked their identities as real US residents by using

---

[48] Indictment at 6, *United States v. Internet Research Agency et al.*, No.-1:18-cr-00032-DLF (D.C., filed 16 February 2018).

[49] Ibid., pp. 2 and 6.

[50] See T. Maurer (2018), pp. 58-61.

[51] Indictment at 4, *United States v. Internet Research Agency et al.…*, cit.

[52] Ibid., p. 14.

virtual private networks (VPNs) and the stolen identities of real US citizens[53]. These workers posted about divisive social issues like abortion, gun rights, and immigration. They also spread misinformation, including lies about allegations of voter fraud by the Democratic Party in order to discourage voter turnout in the 2016 election[54].

The IRA also coopted real US citizens to bring its trolling to reality. As the indictment describes, IRA employees contacted political activities using their fake identities and asked them to organise political rallies, such as a "March for Trump," in June 2016. These included a series of rallies in Florida, New York and Pennsylvania. The IRA even went so far as to recruit and pay a person to wear a costume portraying Hillary Clinton in a prison uniform at one of the rallies[55]. And advice from US political activists led the IRA to focus its activities on "purple states," like Colorado, Virginia, and Florida[56]. Additionally, the IRA spread its reach by using powerful social media advertising tools. According to Facebook itself, it found more than 3,000 ads linked to the IRA, which Facebook said reached more than ten million Americans[57].

Finally, the connection between the IRA and the Putin regime is murky. The operation was deniable because of the vague relationship between the Russian government and Yevgeniy Prigozhin and his company, Concord Management. The indictment says that Concord was the IRA's "primary source of funding", paying over US$1.25 million a month for its operations[58]. Prigozhin is a billionaire with extensive contracts with the Russian government and Putin's inner circle[59]. The unclear

[53] Ibid., pp. 16-17.

[54] Ibid., p. 18.

[55] Ibid., p. 27.

[56] Ibid., p. 13.

[57] E. Schrage, "Hard Questions: Russian Ads Delivered to Congress", Facebook press release, 2 October 2017.

[58] Indictment at 6-7, *United States v. Internet Research Agency et al.…*, cit.

[59] N. MacFarquhar, "Yevgeny Prigozhin, Russian Oligarch Indicted by U.S., Is Known as 'Putin's Cook'", *The New York Times*, 16 February 2018.

nature of the IRA's status underscores that deception and uncertainty are key features of information warfare.

## Case study #3: the DNC hack

The hack of the Democratic National Committee and subsequent release of Clinton campaign documents synthesised Russia's political hacking and information warfare strategies. Special Counsel Robert Mueller's July 2018 indictment names 12 Russian military intelligence officers who it says "conducted large-scale cyber operations to interfere with the 2016 US presidential election"[60]. The operation blended the hacking of emails and other internal documents from the DNC, the Democratic Congressional Campaign Committee (DCCC), and the Hillary Clinton campaign with their release over several channels, including the website Wikileaks. As such, it exemplifies how the Russian security services use political hacking to fuel information operations, with the hacked documents providing the material for social media dissemination.

At Putin's direction, beginning in March 2016 the Russia's military intelligence (GRU) officers in Unit 26165 under Commander Viktor Netyksho spearphished Clinton campaign officials and then broke into the DCCC network that April[61]. Netyksho's men installed copies of their X-Agent malware on the DCCC network and used it to steal files to GRU-leased servers. Employing a network of intermediary servers to mask their presence, the GRU surveilled DCCC employees to steal login credentials for the DNC network, thus gaining access[62]. Notably, Trend Micro security researchers had previously detected X-Agent malware in the so-called "Operation Pawn Storm" reported in 2014[63].

---

[60] Indictment at 1, *United States v. Netyksho et al.,* No. 1:18-cr-00215-ABJ, (D.C., filed 13 July 2018).

[61] Indictment at 6-8, *United States v. Netyksho et al...*, cit.

[62] Ibid., pp. 9-10.

[63] L. Sun, B. Hong, and F. Hacquebord, "Pawn Storm Update: iOS Espionage App Found", Trend Micro blog post, 4 February 2015.

Meanwhile, a parallel GRU unit under Alexander Osadchuk began setting up the infrastructure for information operations. These officers created fake online personas to stage the release of these documents, including "Guccifer 2.0" and "DCLeaks". They also contacted a number of organisations, including journalists in the US and the website Wikileaks, offering to provide stolen documents for publication, and ultimately sending thousands of documents to Wikileaks[64]. While this scheme proceeded in the summer of 2016, another officer under Osadchuk's direction, Anatoliy Kovalev also hacked into the website of a state board of election and stole voter data for 500,000 US citizens and targeted state offices responsible for administering elections[65]. This is yet another facet of the GRU's opportunistic hacking. If the GRU had pursued these breaches further, they could have turned them toward public release as well.

Returning to Netyksho's hacking scheme, by May 2016 his men had stolen thousands of emails from DNC employees and exfiltrated these and other documents to GRU-leased servers in the US, paid for with Bitcoin[66]. The next step was to put them to use. The indictment documents how one of Netykhsho's men, Alexsey Lukashev, used the same email account associated with spearphishing operations to register the "dcleaks.com" website[67]. Stolen emails from the DNC and Clinton campaign the GRU posted on DCLeaks got over one million page views over the course of a year.

Social media was the GRU's preferred means of distributing the hacked documents. They set up fake Facebook accounts pretending to be real US citizens and a Twitter account for DCLeaks. The infamous "Guccifer 2.0" persona was another deception effort to stage document releases[68]. These were not ironclad efforts, indeed, as many US analysts concluded at the

[64] Indictment at 13, 17, *United States v. Netyksho et al....*, cit.

[65] Ibid., p. 26.

[66] Ibid., pp. 10-11.

[67] Ibid., p. 13.

[68] Ibid., pp. 14-17.

time that the account was not credible[69]. But it was enough to sow confusion and get the leaked documents into the public view, just like Russia's other information warfare efforts had done. As the public skepticism about Guccifer 2.0 increased, the officers turned to another strategy: coopting outside organisations. Wikileaks reached out to Guccifer 2.0 in June 2016, and the officers saw an opportunity to use Wikileaks as another platform for document release. They ultimately transferred 50,000 documents to Wikileaks, which acted as their willing partner and released nearly all the documents by 7 November 2016, the day before Election Day, without any acknowledged connection back to Guccifer 2.0[70].

The US intelligence community has linked the choice to use document dumps to Russian President Vladimir Putin's perception that the US used the Panama papers and Olympic doping scandal as weapons against Russia. The 2017 intelligence community assessment says Putin, "sought to use disclosures to discredit the image of the United States and cast it as hypocritical"[71].

## Conclusion

Moscow's interference in the 2016 US election was a watershed moment in history for various reasons. Putting aside its implications for domestic politics in the US and international affairs more broadly, it was an important wake-up call for Western countries to revisit their assumptions about Russia's view and behaviour with respect to cyberspace. Moscow's behaviour leading up to the election highlighted that its doctrines'

[69] L. Franceschi-Bicchierai, "Why Does DNC Hacker 'Guccifer 2.0' Talk Like This?", *Motherboard*, 23 June 2016.

[70] Indictment at 18-19, *United States v. Netyksho et al....*, cit.

[71] Office of the Director of National Intelligence, "Assessing Russian Activities and Intentions in Recent US Elections", Intelligence Community Assessment, ICA 2017-01D, 6 January 2017, p. 1.

explicit focus on information security was not hyperbole or propaganda but a comprehensive approach viewing using information operations and cyber operations as an integrated concept. Domestically, the Russian government has translated this approach into a multi-pronged effort to control information, primarily by gaining control over media organisations. Internationally, Moscow has shown an ability to employ different techniques flexibly to maximise its impact. Furthermore, to achieve its desired political objective, the Russian government relies not only on capabilities of its own military and intelligence agencies but engages non-state hackers. Paired with the Internet's ability to achieve these effects remotely and at scale, this unique set of circumstances pose significant conceptual and practical challenge for policy makers in Western capitals.

# 3. China and Cyber: The Growing Role of Information in Chinese Thinking

Dean Cheng

The rise of the People's Republic of China (PRC) over the past four decades has been due, in part, to China's ability to harness the rise of the Information Age for its own purposes. Chinese leaders since Deng Xiaoping opened China to the outside world, recognising that for China to compete successfully, it must be able to exploit advances in modern technology. China's opening and subsequent rise have occurred in the midst of the Information Revolution. At the same time, controlling information has become a central part of China's internal and external security calculations.

This evolving view of the relationship between information and power has crystallised in the past half-century, as the world economy has globalised, and as information has become even more integrated with development. Beginning in the 1970s, the proliferation of microelectronics, computers, and telecommunications technology has accelerated the ability to gather, store, manage, and transmit information. Information technology, including computers and telecommunications systems, has permeated all aspects of society and economies and become an integral part of a nation's infrastructure[1]. Chinese analysts have dubbed this process "informationisation (*xinxihua*; 信息化)".

[1] Tan Wen Fang, "The Impact of Information Technology on Modern Psychological Warfare", *National Defense Science and Technology*, no. 5, 2009, pp. 72-76.

From the Chinese perspective,

> Informationisation is a comprehensive system of systems, where the broad use of information technology is the guide, where information resources are the core, where information networks are the foundation, where information industry is the support, where information talent is a key factor, where laws, policies, and standards are the safeguard[2].

In the face of this broad trend of economic, political, and social informationisation, Chinese analysts have concluded that threats to national interests and security have also become informationised.

The spread of information technology means that potential adversaries have unprecedented access to each other's national economy, as well as the broader population and the top decision-makers. Just as the bomber and long-range missile allow an opponent to directly strike a nation without having to first break through ground or naval defences, information technology similarly outflanks traditional military forces. The proliferation of information technology into society and economics makes them vulnerable to a range of new pressures and threats.

These threats extend beyond information networks (e.g., vulnerability to denial of service attacks) and component computers (e.g., computer viruses, malware). Instead, the very information itself can constitute a threat, if, for example, its content erodes the morale of key decision-makers, popular support for a conflict, or the will of the military to fight. Consequently, China's interpretation of its national interests has expanded, in step with the expanding impact of information writ large on China.

This growing importance of information technology inevitably influences the nature of warfare. Informationised societies and economies lead to informationised wars, which in turn

[2] State Council Information Office, Tenth Five Year Plan for National Economic and Social Development, Informationization Key Point Special Plans, 18 October 2002, http://www.cia.org.cn/information/information_01_xxhgh_3.htm

require informationised militaries to fight them successfully. This reflects the interplay between the military and the larger economy and society. Mechanised military forces are a reflection of the Industrial Age, including both industrial economics and an industrialised society. Correspondingly, there can be no informationised military without an informationised society and economy, and vice versa. In the Chinese view, the People's Liberation Army (PLA) and broader security establishment must be prepared for "informationised warfare (*xinxihua zhanzheng*; 信息化战争)".

In December 2004, Hu Jintao, in his role as chairman of the Central Military Commission, gave a major speech wherein he charged the PLA with a set of "historic missions for the new phase of the new century", commonly referred to as the "new historic missions". The speech essentially provided guidance for what the PLA should be preparing for, given changes in the international strategic context and national development. One of the new historic missions was to "provide strong strategic support for maintaining the nation's interests". While those interests still centre on issues of territorial integrity and national sovereignty, they now also extend to outer space and the electromagnetic spectrum, and into the information domain[3].

## China's Increasing Informationisation

As early as the 1980s, the People's Republic of China began to pay attention to information technology. This was one of the original seven focal areas for Plan 863, the Chinese National High-Technology Research and Development Plan established in 1986, which sought to promote and accelerate Chinese capabilities in key technological areas[4]. Initial efforts in this domain

---

[3] Z. Weiping and L. Minfu, *Discussions on the Military's New Historic Missions*, Beijing, People's Armed Police Publishing House, 2005, p. 138.

[4] For further discussion of the creation of Plan 863, see E. Feigenbaum, *China's Techno-Warriors*, Stanford CA, Stanford University Press, 2003, esp. pp. 141-43.

included promoting fiber-optic technology in order to facilitate the creation of a Chinese information superhighway, as well as the development of large-scale parallel and distributed computing and symmetrical multiprocessing[5]. China also promoted its own personal computers, the "Legend" brand.

As information technology rapidly advanced throughout the 1990s, China's leaders recognised its growing impact and sought to ensure that China would not be left behind. In 1991, China first joined the Internet, as the Institute of High Energy Physics leased a direct international line to the United States[6]. Indeed, Jiang Zemin pushed for China to establish a broader presence on the Internet, at that point still an entity largely limited to the United States. In Jiang's view, it was essential that China be plugged into the global information network if it was to sustain its modernisation efforts.

China's information networks, in terms of both international and domestic connectivity, steadily grew throughout the 1990s. Information technology and informationisation were incorporated into the Ninth Five Year Plan (1996-2000), emphasising the construction of China's telecommunications infrastructure. This included domestic digital mobile communications equipment and program-controlled switchboards. China's networks would be assembled from Chinese-manufactured hardware.

The Chinese simultaneously introduced a series of information programs, part of the "Golden projects", to push Chinese information exploitation forwards. These included:

- Golden Bridge (*jinqiao*; 金桥): an information infrastructure to facilitate the movement of economic information;
- Golden Card (*jinka*; 金卡): a nation-wide payment system promoting the use of credit and debit cards in what had been a cash-driven economy;

[5] E. Feigenbaum (2003), pp. 175 and 181.

[6] G. Austin, *Cyber Policy in China*, Malden MA, Polity, 2014, p. 33.

- Golden Tax (*jinshui*; 金税): computerisation of the nation's tax system, to reduce fraud and tax dodging while simplifying tax payments[7].

It was also during this period that the Chinese "Golden Shield (*jindun*; 金盾)" project was initiated. While China was interested in joining the global telecommunications network, it nonetheless sought to control what could be accessed. Even as China was taking its first steps into connectivity, research was underway to ensure that those connections were firmly under the control and supervision of the Chinese Communist Party (CCP) and its censors. The Golden Shield project, popularly known as "the Great Firewall of China", constituted an initial step of defending the PRC from unauthorised information proliferation from without – and within.

Informationisation is based on more than technology, however. As information was increasingly emphasised, new bureaucracies arose and industries were reorganised. Chinese informationisation efforts were guided by the slogan of "Thorough planning, national leadership; unified standards, joint construction; mutual linkages, shared resources". This reflected efforts to standardise and unify Chinese information technology, increasing compatibility and reducing duplication. In 1998, the Ministry of Information Industries (MII) was organised to supervise China's information industry development.

In 2002, at the 16th Party Congress, informationisation was formally recognised as essential to the growing Chinese "comprehensive national power (*zonghe guojia liliang*; 综合国家力量)". General Secretary Jiang Zemin emphasised the Chinese path to industrialisation and economic modernisation would depend on the information sector. Jiang noted that information technology was the "logical choice" if Chinese industrialisation

[7] C. Zhen-wei Qiang, *China's Information Revolution*, Washington D.C., World Bank Publications, 2007, p. 93; and Guo Liang, *Under the Golden 'Shine': China's Effort to Bridge Government and Citizens*, Beijing, Chinese Academy of Social Sciences, January 2006, pp. 4-6.

was to accelerate, especially since informationisation would generate other benefits, including raising the overall level of scientific and technical awareness, reducing resource consumption, and developing Chinese human resources. Therefore, "we must give priority to the development of the information industry and apply IT in all areas of economic and social development"[8].

As Hu Jintao rose to the top leadership positions in 2002 and 2004, the Chinese leadership shifted gears on broader economic policies. Hu and his premier Wen Jiabao were far less enamored of economic reform than their predecessors Jiang Zemin and Zhu Rongji. Nonetheless, they recognised the importance of expanding the role of information technology in the PRC.

In 2005, the Chinese government promulgated the "National Strategy for Informationization Development, 2006-2020". This charted a course for China's efforts to expand and deepen information technology. Major priorities would be increasing the level of informationisation in the national economy and society; expanding information and communications infrastructure (e.g., making broadband more widely available); promoting the application of information technology in healthcare, education, and government operations; and improving Chinese global competitiveness in information-related technology production, including development of more sophisticated computer programs and applications. Chinese information security systems would meanwhile be strengthened, and informationisation of public security ministries would be enhanced.

Over the next several years, bureaucratic reorganisations reflected the growing emphasis on information technology in both economic and security terms. The Chinese leadership was clearly intent on expanding the PRC's comprehensive national power, which could only happen if information technologies were incorporated and integrated into the broader society. This is the essence of informationisation, from the Chinese perspective.

[8] Jiang Zemin, Work Report to the 16th Party Congress, Xinhua, 17 November 2002.

These efforts to both grow China's information and communications technology (ICT) and limit its impact have redoubled under Xi Jinping. In his speech before the 19th Party Congress, for example, Xi specifically mentioned the effort to "promote further integration of the Internet, big data, and artificial intelligence with the real economy"[9].

These efforts have borne steady fruit, as China's presence on the Internet and level of computerisation have steadily expanded. In 2000, according to the International Telecommunications Union (ITU), China had an Internet usage penetration of less than two percent, with some 22.5 million users in a population of 1.28 billion. This had more than doubled by 2002, to 59 million users, representing 4.6% penetration[10]. By December 2017, the China Internet Network Information Center (CNNIC) was reporting some 772 million Chinese Internet users, marking a 55.8% penetration rate. CNNIC also reports that much of China accesses the Internet via their mobile phones (the foremost means of Internet connectivity in the PRC)[11]. China is clearly on the path towards becoming an information society.

## China's Strategic Approach to Information

Given the importance of information networks to all aspects of comprehensive national power, in the Chinese view, it is not surprising that China has adopted an equally comprehensive approach towards the strategic management of information. This is essential, if one is to achieve "information dominance (*zhi xinxi quan*; 制信息权)", the ability to control information and information flow at a particular time and within a

---

[9] Xi Jinping, "Full Text of Xi Jinping's Report at the 19h CPC National Congress", *China Daily*, 4 November 2017.

[10] Internet World Stats, "China: Internet Usage Stats and Population Report", 2010.

[11] Xinhua, "China's Online Population Hits 772 Mln: Report", *China Daily*, 31 January 2018.

particular space[12]. It entails the ability to collect more information, manage it faster, and employ it more precisely than the adversary[13]. By achieving information dominance, in the Chinese view, one can maximise the effects of all this newly available information. The side that enjoys information dominance can then seize and retain the initiative, and force the adversary into a reactive mode, losing the ability to influence the outcome of an engagement. This exploits a key difference between the mechanised warfare of the Industrial Age, and the informationised warfare of the Information Age. "Mechanised warfare focuses on physically and materially destroying an opponent, whereas informationised warfare focuses on inducing the collapse of the opponent's psychology and will"[14].

Establishing information dominance involves efforts that span from the strategic to the tactical level. The knowledge required to establish information dominance includes an understanding of not only the adversary's information systems, but also their key decision-makers and decision-making processes. This entails significant intelligence gathering throughout peacetime. Because of the rapid, decisive nature of "local wars under informationised conditions", it is not possible to wait until the formal commencement of hostilities to begin preparations. At a minimum, identifying opposition capabilities and weaknesses must be undertaken in peacetime.

Nor can establishing information dominance be solely a military function. As the world has informationised, so has the global economy; consequently, key vulnerabilities may not be in the military systems, but in the financial system or critical

---

[12] All Army Military Terminology Management Commission, *Chinese People's Liberation Army Terminology*, unabridged volume, Beijing, Military Science Publishing House, 2011, p. 79.

[13] *PLA Encyclopedia*, Chinese Military Encyclopedia 2nd Edition Editorial Committee, *Military Strategy*, Beijing, China Encyclopedia Publishing House, 2007, p. 68.

[14] Fan Gaoming, "Public Opinion Warfare, Psychological Warfare, and Legal Warfare, the Three Major Combat Methods to Rapidly Achieving Victory in War", *Global Times*, 8 March 2005.

infrastructures such as power or transportation. Because modern information networks are interconnected, and given their extensive permeation, "information dominance" involves gaining access not only to enemy military networks but to essential non-military ones as well. Civilian and commercial decision-makers and the broader population are also vital targets. Similarly, it is essential to target not only an adversary's data, but also the systems involved in data collection and management, and the users and analysts of that data as well.

For the Chinese leadership, then, establishing information dominance entails influencing global Internet governance, managing information flows to and within China, and undertaking political warfare measures, which is the weaponisation of information at the strategic level.

## China's challenge to the current Internet governance

The first layer of China's strategic approach to information is the concept of Internet sovereignty. Senior Chinese officials regularly reiterate Beijing's longstanding calls for extending national sovereignty across the Internet. For the Chinese leadership, only by altering the international Internet governance structure, revising underlying assumptions, and gaining acceptance of "Internet sovereignty" can China defend itself from Internet-borne threats to information control. By delegitimising the free flow of information, Chinese authorities would justify efforts to control what information can flow across state boundaries, and could even seek assistance from other states in constricting that flow.

From Beijing's perspective, determining who has a voice in managing the Internet is vital, as that can limit who can access the Internet. For the Chinese leadership, Internet governance is a reflection of national authority and power. The Chinese argue that Internet management should be limited to nation-states, reiterating this position in various official documents, such as the "National Strategy for Informationization Development, 2006-2020" and the 2010 Chinese white paper on the Internet, as well as speeches by officials such as Lu Wei and Xi Jinping.

As important as the ability to authorise Internet names and addresses is also the ability to manage a strategic resource, since those names and addresses determine how one accesses the Internet (and how others access you). Given its importance, the ability to authorise Internet names and addresses cannot be left in the hands of foreigners[15]. Nor can it be lightly granted to non-state actors who might challenge Beijing's authority.

There are a host of entities that the CCP has sought to mute and does not want to have unfettered access to the Internet. For example, it does not want to cede any kind of cyberspace naming authority to Taiwan. Indeed, one Chinese consideration about Internet governance is its desire to restrict the online voice of the authorities in Taipei, to ensure that they have no more prospect of international support in cyberspace than they do in the current political environment. As troubling for the CCP is the ability of groups such as the Tibetan government in exile or Falun Gong to voice adversarial positions and challenges to Beijing via the Internet.

This Chinese interest in preserving national sovereignty on the Internet, including maintaining control over how "China" is represented in cyberspace, has led to fundamental antagonism towards the current structure of Internet governance. When the Internet first began to grow beyond a handful of educational and governmental institutions, the United States vested its administration in the Internet Corporation for Assigned Names and Numbers (ICANN), a non-profit entity. In essence, since its establishment in 1998, ICANN has had the authority to determine who can obtain the unique identifiers, or IP addresses, that allow others to access one's information on the World Wide Web.

ICANN policy has been grounded in the "multi-stakeholder" model. This system seats governments alongside other elements of global society, including academia, business, civil society

[15] Zhang Weihua, "New Theories of Dominance: Issues Concerning Information Dominance", *Journal of Information*, no. 12, 2007, p. 59.

(e.g., religions, non-governmental organisations), and industry, managing the Internet as a whole through a consensus-based process. Individuals, as well as larger organised groups, are represented, none of them enjoying a privileged place at the table. The objective is to sustain the Internet as a borderless realm, where information flows freely.

Not surprisingly, the Chinese have opposed this multi-stakeholder approach, preferring a much more state-centred one. Ideally, from Beijing's perspective, Internet governance should be exercised primarily by governments, who would establish the rules for Internet activity, including the ability to apportion Internet addresses (and generally manage its activity) within their national borders. In short, state sovereignty would be extended to cyberspace. China objects to ICANN at a fundamental level – a state-centric governance model can hardly be managed by a non-state actor, much less one that views other non-state elements as co-equals.

Given these problems, the Chinese, as well as other authoritarian states such as Russia, have wanted to see Internet governance transferred from ICANN to the ITU, an agency of the United Nations. China formally proposed this at the 2005 UN-sponsored World Summit on the Information Society (WSIS). In September 2011, China and Russia, along with Tajikistan and Uzbekistan, submitted a proposal for an "International Code of Conduct on Information Security" to the UN Security Council that would enlarge the role of the ITU at the expense of ICANN[16].

Meanwhile, Chinese authorities have sought to undermine the multi-stakeholder approach in other ways. There are five Regional Internet Registries (RIR), which help in the assignment of IP addresses. The RIRs (one each for Africa, Asia, North and South America, and Europe) are private not-for-profit corporations, like ICANN. Within the Asia-Pacific

[16] "Letter Dated 12 September 2011 from the Permanent Representatives of China, the Russian Federation, Tajikistan, and Uzbekistan to the United Nations Addressed to the Secretary-General", 14 September 2011.

Network Information Center (APNIC) purview are several National Internet Registries (NIR), intended to address unique national requirements. These NIRs are also authorised to issue IP addresses and register names, like the RIRs and ICANN in general.

The Chinese NIR, the CNNIC, however, has sought to control the issuance of addresses within China, pressing Chinese companies and Internet Service Providers (ISPs) to go through themselves, rather than through the APNIC. In 2004, Houlin Zhao, then the Director of the ITU's Telecommunications Standardization Bureau, pushed for national authorities to manage the allocation of at least a portion of the new IPv6 (Internet Protocol version 6) addresses, rather than relying on the RIRs[17]. Zhao, who has since risen to Secretary-General of the ITU, acknowledges that he has a different vision for Internet governance, noting that ITU is often seen as pursuing a more top-down approach[18].

## Managing China's information access

For the Chinese leadership, establishing information dominance also requires preventing an adversary from exercising undue influence on the population. In the Information Age, this means that Chinese authorities must control the flow of information to the Chinese people, including via traditional media, but especially across the Internet and through social media channels.

---

[17] IPv6 addresses were developed to meet growing demand for Internet addresses, as the previous IPv4 pool, was being exhausted. IPv6 addresses are also expected to be more secure. P. Hermann-Seaton, *Security Features in IPv6*, SANS Institute Reading Room, 2002; M. Mueller, "China and Global Internet Governance: A Tiger by the Tail", in R. Deibert, J. Palfrey, R. Rohozinski, and J. Zittrain (eds.), *Access Contested: Security, Identity, and Resistance in Asian Cyberspace*, Cambridge, MA, MIT Press, 2011, p. 185.

[18] M. Ermert, "ITU Secretary-General Visits Old Arch-Rival IETF", Intellectual Property Watch, 21 July 2015.

At the same time, not only must the CCP counter foreign intrusions and interference, but it must also prevent *domestic* opponents from creating and spreading unrest. Social media platforms especially increase the potential of organised protests against CCP rule. The specter of internal and external opposition combining, or worse cooperating, makes information control a paramount priority, and unfettered information flow a *strategic* threat.

The confluence of information technology expansion and the collapse of the Soviet Union affects CCP threat perceptions. After all, China's first connection to the Internet in 1994 occurred in the shadow of the USSR's collapse, which itself came on the heels of the Tiananmen Square massacre. The growing ability to share information, and act upon it, clearly poses burgeoning challenges to a Chinese leadership that has witnessed the collapse of global Communist ideology and significant domestic unrest. Chinese efforts to control the Internet and social media, with their extensive permeation and reach, should be seen as the equivalent of strategic homeland defence. The CCP's determination to limit the vulnerability of the population (and therefore itself) to information weapons parallels civil defence measures to protect the population from nuclear weapons.

Especially important is control of social media platforms, which not only allow prompt dissemination of information to large audiences (akin to traditional media), but also can rapidly organise public opinion and even action. Indeed, preserving social control and preventing the population from engaging in unapproved action appears to be as important as censoring information outright. Rebecca MacKinnon observed in 2009 that Chinese governmental regulatory bodies base rewards and punishments "on the extent to which Internet companies successfully prevent groundswells of public conversation around politically inflammatory topics that might inspire a critical mass of people to challenge Communist Party authority"[19].

---

[19] R. MacKinnon, "China's Censorship 2.0: How companies Censor Bloggers",

A subsequent study reached a similar conclusion, observing that "the purpose of the censorship program is to reduce the probability of collective action by clipping social ties whenever any collective movements are in evidence or expected"[20]. Researchers found that Sina Weibo postings and other expressions were far more likely to be taken down, and would be taken down faster, when they promoted collective action, e.g., protests or gatherings. This was true *even if the messages supported the government's position*. "Whether or not the posts are in favour of the government, its leaders, and its policies has no measurable effect on the probability of censorship"[21].

The Chinese government closely monitors not only information but how that information is interpreted and acted upon. While it is not possible to totally control what is expressed, Beijing clearly tries to suppress unauthorised, popular reactions to that expression. The central authorities' efforts are facilitated by the near total dominance of domestic providers, as well as governmental control of China's telecommunications infrastructure. By creating an indigenous set of social media platforms, rather than relying on foreign programs, Beijing can not only control what is transmitted via social media, but also how that information travels over China's information and telecommunications networks. For example, Beijing has been able to shut down text messaging systems while maintaining cellular phone network operations. This has been essential, given the heavy reliance on mobile phones rather than landlines for general internal connectivity. Both private citizens and the government can continue to communicate, even when the government simultaneously clamps down on the ability to organise opposition, but the ability to create crowds is minimised.

---

*First Monday*, vol. XIV, no. 2, 2 February 2009.

[20] G. King, J. Pan, and M.E. Roberts, "How Censorship in China Allows Government Criticism But Silences Collective Expression", *American Political Science Review*, May 2013, p. 1.

[21] Ibid., p. 13.

In sensitive areas such as Tibet and Xinjiang, Chinese authorities have amply demonstrated both will and capability to prevent unauthorised and uncontrolled dissemination of information. In Tibet, both Internet and telephone connectivity has reportedly been spotty and uncertain since 2008 protests. When protests about racial violence against Uighur workers in Guangdong became violent in 2009, Internet access was suspended across the entire Xinjiang Autonomous Region within hours. Limits on phone calls and text messaging followed[22]. Since then, there have been repeated shutdowns and disruptions of Xinjiang Internet and telephone service. However, in both areas, government agencies (e.g., police) and critical infrastructure such as finance and transportation have retained connectivity, reflecting the Chinese ability to wield a scalpel as well as a cleaver when controlling information[23].

Through central control of physical infrastructure and promotion of indigenous software and platforms, China has created a fairly insulated, relatively controlled internal information environment, even as it is connected to the global information network. This is backed by an overlapping array of technical and human censors. These ensure not only that disseminated information is politically acceptable, but any reactions can be channelled into acceptable forms.

The average Chinese citizen's view of the world, and even of China, is bounded by a pervasive, but not necessarily obvious, set of blinders. So long as they stay within those limits, they are free to enjoy the benefits of both an extensive internal information network, as well as access to broader global resources. But should Beijing deem it necessary, the authorities can close some or even all of those shutters, in ways that few other authoritarian states can, because all of the levers are in Chinese hands.

---

[22] "Is China Fraying?", *The Economist*, 9 July 2009.

[23] O. Lam, "China: When the Network Was Cut in Xinjiang", *Global Voices Advocacy*, 13 October 2010.

## Government limitation of the Internet

While China's opening to the West forced it to accommodate greater media access, this was nonetheless controllable. The Central Propaganda Department has long been an established mechanism for press censorship, so it could readily accommodate changes in the traditional media environment, including greater foreign presence. Indeed, even with the introduction of foreign journalists, there were still only a restricted number of outlets. The number of persons and entities that required monitoring remained limited. Previous media access controls (e.g., press passes, visas) remained sufficient to limit the newly expanded foreign press.

By contrast, the Internet poses an unprecedented threat to the governmental ability to control information flows. This is in part because the CCP wants China to have broad access to the Internet. It is a key means of conducting business; China could not hope to participate in the modern global economy if it did not have ready connectivity with global information networks. It also easily accesses the global wealth of knowledge, an essential means for improving China at relatively low cost.

But access is a two-way street. Expanding linkage to the global information network raises the potential vulnerability of Chinese networks to significant criminal activity. China regularly argues that it is among the most-hacked nations in the world. In 2012, for example, the Chinese reported that 22,000 phishing websites had targeted Chinese netizens, while 14 million mainframes in China had been hijacked by various Trojan horses and botnets. Many of these are traced to foreign websites, "with the United States being the largest source of such hacking activities"[24].

Moreover, just as Chinese authorities use the Internet to obtain information and to influence others, other players, including both state and non-state adversaries, can use it to transmit

---

[24] "China's Cyber Security Under Severe Threat: Report", Xinhua, 19 March 2013.

information to Chinese audiences. Senior Chinese leaders including Deng Xiaoping, Jiang Zemin, and Hu Jintao have all warned of Western efforts to subvert China through "westernisation" and "peaceful evolution", i.e., eroding CCP legitimacy (leading to "peaceful evolution" away from CCP rule). As one observer astutely notes, *the entire basis* of the past three decades of Chinese economic reform has been

> to benefit from Western technology and from trade with the global market economy *without* converging into the West's liberal democratic governance model[25].

Chinese authorities consider efforts to draw China into that Western model, whether conscious or not, a *de facto* form of political warfare. The introduction of the Internet only exacerbates them.

If the Chinese leadership is going to prevent an opponent from effectively applying various forms of information against the population and leadership, it must be able to control information flows across the Internet. Indeed, because the whole purpose of the Internet is to disseminate information, it constitutes a major challenge to central government efforts to maintain control, even as it helps stimulate Chinese economic development by facilitating information sharing and access. Consequently, substantial sums and effort have been invested in controlling potential adversary access to the Chinese population and senior military and civilian leadership. These efforts coincide with a broader interest in maintaining control over the Chinese population, given the omnipresent risk of unrest. Managing this threat to regime control has therefore entailed highest level attention and a multi-layered approach.

One key part of the Chinese effort to control the Internet is the China Cyberspace Administration, also known as the State Internet Information Office (SIIO). Xi Jinping has made clear that the SIIO would play a key role in not only administering

---

[25] M. Mueller (2011), p. 190.

the Internet in China, but would be able to "investigate and punish websites violating laws and regulations"[26]. In August 2014, governmental circular noted that the SIIO's roles and responsibilities includes the healthy and orderly development of the Internet, protection of the citizenry, and maintenance of national security and public interest[27].

## Domestic legal controls on the Internet

Supporting the efforts of the SIIO, the Chinese have been steadily creating a domestic legal and regulatory framework that firmly extends the state's grip over all parts of China's internal cyber community. This effort began almost as soon as China linked to the Internet, and even before commercial access was made available to the broader Chinese public. In February 1994, the State Council issued State Council Order 147, "Regulations for the Safety Protection of Computer Information Systems". This vested the Ministry of Public Security (MPS) with responsibility for supervising computer information in China[28]. This was further supplemented by State Council Order 195, issued in February 1996, which listed specific Internet governance regulations. Beijing has since issued an array of regulations, laws, and directives discouraging "inappropriate" use of the Internet and its information.

Chinese efforts to restrict foreign access likely gained impetus after the 2013 revelations about American cyber-espionage by Edward Snowden. In 2014, the Chinese government reportedly excluded foreign anti-virus companies Symantec and Kaspersky from bidding on Chinese government contracts[29].

---

[26] "China Sets Up Office for Internet Information Management", Xinhuanet, 4 May 2011.

[27] State Council, "Notification of the State Council on Authorizing the State Internet Information Office for Responsibility Regarding Internet Information and Content Management", State Council Information Office, 26 August 2014.

[28] Open Net Initiative, "Internet Filtering in China in 2004-2005: A Country Study", 14 April 2005.

[29] J. Finkle, "Beijing to Bar Kaspersky, Symantec Anti-Virus in Procurement:

Central government efforts to control information flows are not solely aimed at users. ISPs, cyber-cafes, and other access providers are also closely scrutinised. The State Council has issued various regulations to govern online businesses. ISPs and Internet Content Providers (ICPs) were licensed by the Ministry of Information Industry (MII), and now by the Ministry of Industry and Information Technology (MIIT), which absorbed MII in 2008. ISPs are also expected to adhere to the "Public Pledge on Self-Discipline for China's Internet Industry", and are "encouraged" to join the Internet Society of China, a governmentally backed "non-governmental organisation" which disseminates the latest guidelines on censored topics, terms, etc[30].

These entities and pledges help promote "self-regulation". Private companies such as ISPs are expected to enforce legal requirements, whether use of Chinese software for information security, or monitoring their own traffic and networks for dangerous or malicious behaviour. ISPs, cyber-cafes, and other providers are responsible for ensuring that all users register with their real names, a centerpiece of many Chinese efforts to limit anonymity on the Chinese Internet. At the same time, as will be discussed below, ISPs also are part of the human censor network that backstops technical censorship methods.

As cybersecurity is more explicitly linked to national security, pressure on these companies will grow. Article 25 of the 2015 Chinese National Security Law specifies that the state's national security responsibilities include maintaining national network and information security, stopping "unlawful and criminal activity", including "dissemination of unlawful and harmful information", as well as "maintaining cyberspace sovereignty, security, and development interests". It specifically includes national security reviews and oversight management of "Internet

Report", *Reuters*, 3 August 2014.

[30] S. Arsene, "The Impact of China on Global Internet Governance in an Era of Privatized Control", Paper presented at the 10th Annual Chinese Internet Research Conference, May 2012.

information technology products and services"[31]. The censors employed by many ISPs and other cyber companies are kept busy by these requirements.

Meanwhile, the Chinese cybersecurity law that came into effect on 1 January 2016, further complicates matters. This legislation does not require foreign companies to keep local user data in China, and did not require installation of government-accessible backdoors in software (as had been proposed in earlier drafts). It *does* require all telecommunications and Internet companies doing business in China to cooperate with Chinese law enforcement and security organisations. This includes controlling information flows in defence of cyberspace sovereignty, as well as information network security and development efforts. The legislation requires all companies to provide "technical assistance," including decryption of user data, in support of "counter-terrorism" activities[32].

## Human and technological means of limiting access

While Chinese diplomats strive to extend national sovereignty to cyberspace, and Chinese legislators and Party officials design legal controls over domestic Internet behaviour, Chinese engineers have sought to technologically limit and monitor data flowing into China. This is facilitated by Beijing's limiting connections to the broader global information networks (and therefore global access into China). Fiber optic cables enter China at only three point – the Beijing-Tianjin region; Shanghai; and Guangzhou. There are only a limited number of Internet exchange points (IXPs) running via these cables, mostly controlled by the Chinese government. This leads to congestion and a slower Internet speed for Chinese users accessing the outside world, but eases the government's ability to monitor traffic entering and leaving China.

---

[31] "People's Republic of China National Security Law", *China Daily*, 1 July 2015.

[32] B. Einhorn, "A Cybersecurity Law in China Squeezes Foreign Tech Companies", *Bloomberg News*, 21 January 2016.

As important, the Chinese government has long supported research in additional programs and measures that limit information flows. The 2000 decision on preserving computer network security charges the government at all levels to "support research and development of the technology for computer network security and enhance the ability of maintaining security of the network" [33]. A high priority has been filtering foreign content, both in terms of what outsiders can send into China, but also what Chinese netizens can access.

A centerpiece of this effort is the "Great Firewall of China" (GFWC). This "on-path" system is the first line of technical defence, monitoring traffic across the three portals that link the Chinese portion of the Internet to the rest of the world. It also has some capacity to monitor internal Chinese computer activity, although this is sometimes conflated with the "Golden Shield" project, which is more focused on monitoring domestic Chinese online behaviour. The avowed purpose of the GFWC is to keep outsiders from being able to attack Chinese Internet users. In reality, the GFWC has demonstrated an ability to censor websites and even individual web pages and images, limiting Chinese citizens' ability to access the global Internet. Theoretically, the GFWC could shut down connectivity between China and the rest of the global Internet entirely, if necessary.

The GFWC employs a variety of methods to prevent Chinese netizens from accessing information that might contradict or challenge the government's preferred line. IP addresses may be blocked, or attempts to connect to them may be misdirected. In addition, in a different application of typical intrusion detection systems, the GFWC undertakes data inspection and filtering to examine Uniform Resource Locators (URLs), or web addresses, as well as the numeric IP addresses. It can also examine actual content, in order to more precisely filter out individual web pages and images.

---

[33] The Central People's Government of the People's Republic of China, "Decision of the Standing Committee of the National People's Congress on Preserving Computer Network Security", 28 December 2000.

The GFWC's purpose is not simply to block content and limit access to forbidden sites; it also seeks to make such content and access more complicated and frustrating, so that users will avoid them. Thus, the GFWC typically tries to limit the degree to which its censorship is noticeable to the average user. While the GFWC will block access to some websites (or even individual pages or images), it does not necessarily interfere with access to other parts of the Internet. A user may therefore not realise that their search has been blocked, but may instead assume that a website is no longer operating or is being modified.

The GFWC is meant to complement various other measures, such as real-name registration and human censors, as well as broader laws and pronouncements regarding unacceptable or dangerous behaviour (not just online), to discourage efforts to access forbidden information. It is estimated, for example, that less than 10% of China's netizens engage in political discourse on the Internet at all[34]. Although this remains an enormous number (since China has over 700 million users), this nonetheless makes censorship and information control more manageable.

Not surprisingly, a number of efforts have emerged to try to circumvent the GFWC, which in turn have led to Chinese government counter-countermeasures. For example, Chinese and foreign computer users have tried to foster "virtual private networks" (VPN) to allow less fettered access to the global Internet. VPNs establish secure connections between a user's computer and a separate network, so that the user's computer is treated as though it were part of that local network (even if it is physically separated). One can then access any information that the local network might contain.

Chinese authorities began to develop tools to crack down on the use of VPNs as soon as they began to gain popularity. Some commercial VPN sites were entirely blocked. Another counter

[34] T. Lum, P. Moloney Figliola, and M. Weed, *China, Internet Freedom, and US Policy*, R42601, Washington D.C., Congressional Research Service, 2012, p. 1.

to established VPN connections was emplaced in 2012, with updates to the GFWC allowing it to "learn, discover, and block VPN protocols automatically"[35]. It is believed that, through "deep packet inspection", the GFWC can at least determine whether packets are encrypted, even if their content remains inaccessible to the censors. If a substantial amount of encrypted traffic is detected bound for a particular network, the GFWC may then block that path.

By 2014, commercial VPN companies that serve Chinese clients reported even more extensive interference with their services[36]. Whereas earlier versions had blocked OpenVPN, the least sophisticated tunneling protocol, further upgrades to the GFWC are now apparently affecting more advanced tunneling protocols, such as PPTP (Point-to-Point Tunneling Protocol) and SSh2 (Secure Shell-2), making it increasingly harder to establish and maintain VPN connections through the GFWC. China officially banned the use of "unauthorised" VPNs, effective March 2018, but it is unclear, as of this writing, exactly which entities are affected by this ban.

Chinese oversight of its Internet is further supported through an army of human censors. Recognising that human ingenuity, coupled with current events, is likely to outpace automated search systems' ability to curtail dissemination of forbidden information, the Chinese authorities have created a network of human censors to further enforce restrictions.

The human censorship effort relies heavily on the ISPs. Because the Chinese government holds to the position of "intermediary liability," that is, "one is responsible for what one publishes", Chinese ISPs are incentivised to limit potential posting or discussion of forbidden topics[37]. As a result, not only have most ISPs installed various filtering systems to detect (and

---

[35] "Great Firewall 'Upgrade' Troubles VPN Users in China", *AFP*, 21 December 2012.

[36] S. Yan, "China Crackdown Makes It Harder to Get Around Great Firewall", *CNN*, 28 January 2015.

[37] S. Arsene (2012).

eliminate) sensitive words and phrases, but they also field teams of employees and volunteers who monitor chat rooms, review blogs and web pages, and otherwise help ensure that what is published via the ISP does not trouble the authorities[38].

These, in turn, are supported by the government's own cyber police. In 2004, this was estimated to already number some 30,000 members[39]. A decade later, reports suggest that China may have 100,000 to two million government censors, tracking both Internet and social media (including microblog) posts and comments[40].

## Government control of social media

The rise of social media poses an additional problem for Chinese efforts to control information flows and dissemination. The proliferation of video and photos further expanded the forms of information now available, while enhancing its credibility. Indeed, social media have become a major part of the Chinese information environment, as much of China's netizenry accesses the Internet via mobile phones and social media platforms. Chinese microblogging sites such as Sina Weibo, Sohu, and Tencent, the PRC counterparts to twitter, have 200 million subscribers[41]. They are the "primary space for Chinese netizens to voice opinion or discuss taboo subjects"[42]. Not surprisingly, this has led to a range of additional controls on information dissemination.

The Chinese leadership appears even more worried about how social media had been exploited by forces for political and

---

[38] Open Net Initiative (2005).

[39] A.S.Y. Cheung and Z. Yun, *An Overview of Internet Regulation in China*, University of Hong Kong Faculty of Law Research Paper no. 2013/040, 21 November 2013, p. 7.

[40] "Cat and Mouse", *The Economist*, 6 April 2013; and "China Employs Two Million Microblog Monitors, State Media Say", *BBC News*, 4 October 2013.

[41] D. Bamman, B. O'Connor, and N. Smith, "Censorship and Deletion Practices in Chinese Social Media", *First Monday*, vol. XVII, no. 3, 5 March 2012.

[42] B. Xu, *Media Censorship in China*, Council on Foreign Relations, 25 September 2014.

social change abroad. Beginning with the "Rose Revolution" in Georgia in 2003, and the subsequent 2004 Ukrainian "Orange Revolution" and 2005 Kyrgyz "Tulip [or Pink] Revolution", a number of former Soviet republics underwent political upheaval. Many protests in these countries were organised through social media such as emails and text messages. Even governmental crackdowns in Arab countries in the face of public protests were often ineffectual, since governments in Cairo and Tunis could not control the social media networks that protestors were exploiting. Companies such as twitter, facebook, etc., were based abroad, and not vulnerable to local pressure. Moreover, governments could not cut off access to social media without also affecting their own connectivity to the global Internet.

To stem such possibilities, the Chinese have extended the comprehensive array of countermeasures against the free flow of information to various social media networks. Rather than eliminating all social media, as in North Korea, the Chinese leadership has instead redirected the public's access to domestic companies, excluding foreign platforms. Just as China's physical information networks would be built from Chinese equipment, China's appetite for social media would be met by Chinese companies.

Today, Chinese computer users search the Internet with Baidu, instead of Google. They share videos through Youku, rather than Youtube, and they don't tweet, they microblog across Sina Weibo and Tencent. Chinese online shoppers browse Taobao, and pay with Alipay. All of these products and platforms are managed by Chinese companies, and while the companies may not be state-owned, they clearly cooperate with censors and submit to broader government control, much like the commercial news media in China. Indeed, as Weibo's public filings at the time of its initial public offering (IPO) noted, failure to comply with government demands for censorship "may subject us to liabilities and penalties and may even result in the temporary blockage or complete shutdown of our online operations"[43]. Consequently, should the Chinese public try to organise themselves as Middle East populations did during the 2009 Iranian Green Movement, 2010 "Jasmine Revolution", and 2011 "Arab Spring", the Chinese authorities have the ability to mute and neutralise such efforts.

## Waging Political Warfare: The Weaponisation of Information

From the Chinese leadership's perspective, the West has been waging an unrelenting series of political attacks on the Chinese Communist Party. This is reflected in the omnipresent threat of "westernisation" and "splittism", endangering the nation's political security and the Party's hold on power. This is at the root of Western calls for greater democratisation and liberalisation. Such calls, and the supporting efforts to promote political liberalisation, are examples, to the Chinese mind of "political warfare (*zhengzhi zhan*; 政治战)", using information to undertake sustained attacks against the enemy's thinking and psychology, to eventually subvert their will[44].

Although political warfare is mainly waged with strategic communications tools, including television, radio, the Internet, and news organisations, it is nonetheless considered *a form of warfare*. It envisions the use of information to attack opponents, eroding will, imposing psychological pressure, and influencing cognitive processes and the framework of perceptions. Because of the informationised condition of the global economy, political warfare efforts are no longer limited to frontline military forces, but are applied against adversary populations and leadership. Political warfare is the weaponisation of soft power.

---

[43] Weibo Corporation, "Form F-1 Registration Statement with US Securities and Exchange Commission", 14 March 2014, p. 36.

[44] Y. Chunchang and S. Hetai, *Political Warfare/Operations Under Informationized Conditions*, Beijing, Long March Press, 2005, p. 15.

Similarly, because modern information technology blurs the lines between peacetime and wartime, between military and civilian, and among strategy, operations, and tactics, political warfare is not limited to when hostilities have formally commenced, and is not focused solely on military targets[45]. Instead, informationised warfare includes activities that are undertaken in peacetime, many of which are aimed at the adversary's political leadership and broad population. Informationised warfare, even more than Industrial-Era mechanised warfare, encompasses the entire society of both sides.

## PLA concepts of political warfare operations

Given the importance of political warfare, it should not be surprising that it is entrusted to the highest bureaucratic levels of the PLA. According to the 2003 "Political Work Regulations of the Chinese People's Liberation Army," and the subsequent 2010 revision, the General Political Department (GPD), one of the four General Departments that ran the PLA, is responsible for the conduct of political warfare. In particular, it is responsible for waging the so-called "three warfares (*san zhan*; 三战)" of public opinion warfare, psychological warfare, and legal warfare, the central methods of political warfare[46].

The "three warfares" will be conducted in combination, as they are an integrated whole. Both individually and in concert, these political warfare efforts strive to shake the enemy's will, question their motives, induce divides and splits within the enemy's ranks, and constrain their activities. While ideally they might cause an opponent to concede the struggle entirely,

[45] Yuan Wenxian, *The Science of Military Information*, Beijing, National Defense University Publishing House, 2008, pp. 77-79.

[46] How the organisational reforms of 2015-2016 will affect the implementation of these regulations is unclear. However, there is a Political Work Department (*zhengzhi gongzuo bu*; 政治工作部) in the new structure, which will likely exercise comparable responsibilities. At the same time, the PLA Strategic Support Force has apparently absorbed at least one element of the former General Political Department, one responsible for the "three warfares".

more likely they will erode an adversary's will, and thus reduce the ability to sustain any resistance to more kinetic operations.

Because of the difficulties in coordinating political warfare efforts with each other, as well as with both broader strategic measures (e.g., economic, diplomatic efforts) and military operations, the Chinese are emphatic about the need for coordination. This includes establishing a coherent plan for its conduct, incorporating not only the elements of political warfare (including the "three warfares"), but also other military, media, political, and diplomatic activities.

PLA efforts at political warfare were simplified and facilitated by vesting it within the GPD (and now the Political Work Department or PWD). Many PWD officers have undergone training in political warfare: indeed, they are specialists. Therefore, they will be planning and implementing operations for which they have been specifically trained. Moreover, the PLA contains an entire PWD chain of command that parallels the operational chain. This allows political warfare practitioners to oversee, coordinate, and integrate political warfare activities from the tactical to the strategic level, while maintaining methodological consistency and focus on specific goals.

The PWD's role also will facilitate coordination between political officers and staff and their operational counterparts of the Joint Staff Department (JSD). Because of the dual-control system (where authority is shared between JSD and PWD, especially through the political committee that runs the unit), there are extensive peacetime, day-to-day links between the two staffs as they manage the unit together.

Taken together, the "three warfares" seek to employ various types of information, e.g., diplomatic, political, economic, as well as military, in a manner consistent with military strategic guidelines and objectives, to win the political initiative and achieve a psychological advantage. The aim is to strengthen one's own resolve while disheartening the adversary, since the lack of will makes even the most sophisticated weaponry irrelevant. An essential element of achieving this psychological advantage is to present oneself as the aggrieved party and holding the moral and legal high ground. Not only does this serve to stiffen one's own will, but it can be an important part of influencing bystanders and third-parties[47]. Political warfare complements, but does not necessarily displace, traditional use of force.

Each of the "three warfares" employs information in a different manner to achieve these goals, but reinforces the other two. Psychological warfare exploits information by drawing upon political, economic, and cultural, as well as military elements of power. Information of each type can serve as a powerful weapon, influencing values, concepts, emotions, and contex[48]. Legal warfare can build psychological support and sympathy among bystanders, and erode an opponent's will by constraining their preferred courses of action for fear of legal repercussions. Public opinion warfare can directly build support, persuading domestic and foreign audiences of the justice of one's own cause and the success of one's own efforts, while undermining an adversary's attempts to do the same. In particular, the growth and expanded reach of media of various sorts makes public opinion warfare especially important, as it can have global effects. Broad domestic and international support, in turn, will generate psychological benefits for oneself and adversely affect the enemy.

## Conclusion

The PRC sees information networks as a truly dual-edged sword. On the one hand, it allows for unprecedented mobility of information, so that knowledge can be rapidly dispersed, facilitating rapid feedback and correction of mistakes. It also provides enormous access to both key political and military

---

[47] Academy of Military Sciences Operations Theory and Regulations Research Department and Informationized Operations Theory Research Office, *Informationized Operations Theory Study Guide*, Beijing, Military Science Publishing House, November 2005, p. 403.

[48] Tan Wen Fang (2009), p. 73.

leaders as well as the broader masses. Networked economies are potentially much more efficient, responsive, and flexible. If the PRC is going to be a major power in the XXI century, it must be part of the global information networks, exploiting the opportunities that have been created.

That same information mobility and wide-ranging access, however, runs counter to the XIX and XX century precepts of political control that still dominate the Chinese leadership – precepts rooted in even older cultural and historical lessons and principles. China may have to access and *participate* in the global information networks, but it is not, and will not be, comfortable *integrating* into those same systems.

Instead, Beijing clearly wishes to establish an unequal information relationship. Chinese leaders want to limit foreign access to Chinese citizens and networks, much as they strive to limit foreign access to Chinese markets. This does not, however, mean that Chinese planners and operators will forego opportunities to exploit the West's greater informational freedom to their own benefit. As important, as they see themselves in a whole-of-society competition with the outside world, Chinese leaders will exploit the entire range of societal tools, from governmental computer network specialists (including both military and non-military elements) to corporate Internet companies, from human censors to artificial intelligence systems, from laws and regulations to bureaucrats seconded to international organisations, to support the Chinese side of that competition.

# 4. North Korean Cyber Threats

Daniel A. Pinkston

North Korean cyber threats pose a number of complicated challenges, some of which are exacerbated by the inter-Korean political and military rivalries. Cyber operations generally are not affected by physical space, but geographic proximity matters on the Korean peninsula. In the case of a crisis or conflict in Korea, escalation dynamics easily could spill across war-fighting domains. Misperception of an adversary's intent, or miscalculation surrounding capabilities and likely outcomes could create strong incentives to strike first in an effort to avoid unacceptable consequences.

Cyberspace is a relatively new domain; international law governing behaviour there is sparse. The dearth of international treaties governing activities in cyberspace means that in the international realm, behaviour is guided by customary law and emerging norms. States can regulate cyber activities within their territory, but this is difficult given the volume of information flows, practically instantaneous transmission, and attribution problems. Regulation also is complicated by the fact that much of the hardware in cyberspace is owned by private firms, many of which have adversarial relationships with governments[1]. Furthermore, even when states can agree on what constitutes

[1] The interests of private information technology (IT) firms and governments can diverge in several ways. For example, firms may wish to protect proprietary information from regulators, or they may wish to withhold information regarding technical failures or data breaches.

illegal or illicit activities in cyberspace, there is no consensus on the role and responsibilities of states for dealing with transgressions that originate in or pass through their territory.

Internet governance is multi-layered with diverse stakeholders from private firms, non-profit organisations, research institutes, technical experts, professional standards associations, national governments, and international organisations. They have different incentives and various types of rule-making authorities. Governance in cyberspace is evolving and some aspects are being challenged. The details of cyberspace governance are beyond the scope of this paper, except to highlight that North Korea and its cyber policies, its emerging capacity, and its intentions will be bound or constrained to some degree by the "nature of cyberspace" and by the other actors within it[2].

At the international level, the International Telecommunication Union (ITU) is responsible for harmonizing technical standards covering the international transmission of information. Relevant private firms can participate in ITU deliberations, but only states have the power to vote on decisions. While the ITU helps resolve coordination problems in setting technical standards, it has neither the capability nor the authority to monitor "illicit or illegal" activities in cyberspace. And when states and non-state actors agree upon what behaviours are unacceptable in cyberspace, enforcement has been relegated to states and domestic law enforcement. The International Court of Justice (ICJ) could adjudicate inter-state cyber disputes, but states have been reluctant or unwilling to seek legal recourse at the ICJ, especially in the case of computer network exploitation (CNE), or espionage, since espionage is a gray area that states have accepted or dealt with through expulsions of diplomats, and through the exchange of spies caught in their territories[3].

---

[2] For background on the actors and rules governing cyberspace, see H. Kwalwasser, "Internet Governance," in F.D. Kramer, S.H. Starr, and L.K. Wentz, *Cyberpower and National Security*, Washington D.C., National Defense University Press, 2009.

[3] G. Brown and K. Poellet, "The Customary International Law of Cyberspace",

State and non-state activities in cyberspace range from cooperative information sharing and communications that enhance efficiencies and make gains from trade possible, to malicious actions such as cyberattacks with kinetic effects. In the middle of the spectrum are vandalism, crime, and espionage. Many of the cyber tools for computer network operations (CNO) can be used for exploitation (exfiltration of data), disruption, vandalism, crime, or computer network attacks (CNA). Therefore, once an unauthorised entity gains access to a computer network, motivation and intention are paramount in final outcomes.

Without a clear international legal framework, norms guide expectations and behaviours, but norms in cyberspace are still emerging. A debate persists over future norms, and over whether they will be more permissive or more restrictive. Pessimists such as Roger Hurwitz argue that international cooperation in the cyber commons will be relatively scarce, while James Forsyth and other scholars assert that the incentives to cooperate will lead states to overcome their collective action problems in cyberspace[4]. Scholars and analysts agree that the emerging environment surrounding cyber governance will be contentious, but they offer different views and predictions about the features of the future cyber regime. For example, Forsyth and Pope provide a realist or statist perspective on cyberspace, describing it as another unexceptional domain subject to great power rivalry. They conclude that as the world evolves from unipolarity to multipolarity, great power rivalry will mirror oligopolistic intensity. While no great power will be able to impose its own preferences for cyber governance, the great powers will still have strong incentives to cooperate in some manner. The rules over the issues of security, individual privacy, legal liability and accountability, and enforcement, etc., will all be

*Strategic Studies Quarterly*, Fall 2012.

[4] R. Hurwitz, "Depleted Trust in the Cyber Commons", *Strategic Studies Quarterly*, Fall 2012; J. Wood Forsyth Jr, "What Great Powers Make It: International Order and the Logic of Cooperation in Cyberspace, *Strategic Studies Quarterly*, Spring 2013.

contested, but some type of governance will emerge because it would be too costly to disconnect from cyberspace[5].

Realists emphasise the power of states to regulate the private sector, and they cite cases of strong state regulation and governments shutting down Internet access or forcing IT firms to turn over data and information to state authorities. However, not all states share the same capacity and resources to monitor and regulate cyberspace within their territories. Mark Raymond argues that the "cyber-regime complex is being shaped by decisions at the global, regional, and domestic levels by international organisations, governments, and the private sector". Accordingly, the future of global Internet governance will not only be the product of a great power compact[6].

Global governance of cyberspace impacts how information, communications and technology (ICT) resources are utilised. The major powers have different perspectives on technical standards, protocols, and legal frameworks. The US and liberal democracies prefer an open and decentralised system, while authoritarian states seek more restrictive standards and protocols. Battles in the ITU, Internet Engineering Task Force (IETF), the Internet Corporation for Assigned Names and Numbers (ICANN), the Internet Assigned Numbers Authority (IANA), and other entities will determine future Internet characteristics with distributional and national security consequences[7].

The global governance of cyberspace matters for the Korean peninsula as it does everywhere else. However, North Korea has been and will continue to be a rule taker in cyberspace. Pyongyang has demonstrated repeatedly that it is willing to violate international norms in numerous areas including

---

[5] J. Wood Forsyth Jr and B.E. Pope, "Structural Causes and Cyber Effects: Why International Order is Inevitable in Cyberspace", *Strategic Studies Quarterly*, Winter 2014.

[6] M. Raymond, "Managing Decentralized Cyber Governance: The Responsibility to Troubleshoot", *Strategic Studies Quarterly*, Winter 2016.

[7] P.A. Yannakogeorgos, "Internet Governance and National Security", *Strategic Studies Quarterly*, Fall 2012.

cyberspace. While North Korea will take advantage of cyber opportunities to further its goals, it is more likely to be a nuisance or act as a spoiler rather than be a positive contributor to cyberspace governance. Whatever type of cyber governance emerges, China and Russia should be expected to play prominent roles with North Korea since most of Pyongyang's access to cyberspace goes through its two neighbours[8]. Much of the debate on Internet governance focuses on the divide over security of data and security of the state versus privacy and individual liberty. Authoritarian states desire more state intervention and control of information while liberal democracies advocate greater privacy and freedom of expression. However, North Korea is an outlier on this spectrum. The ruling Korean Workers Party (KWP) exercises tight control over the dissemination and access to information inside North Korea[9], so Pyongyang has securitised ICT since the advent of cyberspace.

## North Korean ICT Background

The two Koreas have followed very different paths in adopting their ICT infrastructures and their governance of cyberspace. Widespread public access to the Internet and the World Wide Web that began in the 1990s came in the wake of South Korean democratisation and rapid economic growth. Traditional Neo-Confucian norms extolling the value of education helped accelerate the demand for IT services. Furthermore, contemporary South Koreans had witnessed swift social, political,

---

[8] In October 2017, the Russian firm TransTeleCom began routing Internet traffic from North Korea. China Unicom had been the conduit for North Korean Internet access to the outside world since 2010. In October 2017, Russia's TransTeleCom was handling 60% of North Korea's Internet traffic and China Unicom handled 40%. "Russian firm provides new internet connection to North Korea", *Reuters*, 2 October 2017.

[9] For insights into East Asian authoritarian regimes and control of the Internet, see N. Hachigian, "The Internet and Power in One-Party East Asian States", *The Washington Quarterly*, vol. 25, no. 3, Summer 2002, pp. 41-58.

and economic change, so adopting and integrating new ICT hardware and software became just another common aspect of dynamic life in modern South Korea. Almost 100% of South Korean households have Internet access,[10] and the country is well-known for its high-speed Internet service[11].

North Korea trails its South Korean neighbour in almost all economic indicators as well as in indices of public health, democracy, and press freedom[12]. Both sides suffered great losses of life and enormous destruction during the war (1950-1953), but initially, North Korea's mass labour mobilisation and command economy enabled it to outpace the South in the early years of reconstruction. However, Seoul's open economy and export-led growth strategy began to pay off as the South caught up in the 1970s. In the 1980s, the South pulled ahead and the gap has continued to widen since.

Despite Pyongyang's relative economic backwardness, the state has targeted several technologies, particularly those with military applications and those aimed at mitigating the inefficiencies of the command economy. The party and the state also have selected and cultivated the human resources to develop and maintain science and technologies aimed at achieving party goals. For example, in 1977, Kim Il-sung, the "eternal president of the DPRK" said,

> Scientific and technical education should be wholly keyed to [Korean Workers] Party policy. Instruction in all subjects should be based entirely on Party policy and linked to the situation in our country. We should thus make sure that the students learn things that are necessary for our revolution and apply their knowledge and skills in their revolutionary activities[13].

---

[10] E. Ramirez, "Nearly 100% Of Households in South Korea Now Have Internet Access, Thanks to Seniors", *Forbes*, 31 January 2017.

[11] D. Grossman, "South Korea's Already Great Internet Gets Even Greater", *Popular Mechanics*, 11 May 2018.

[12] According to one estimate, South Korea's GDP per capita was US$39,400 in 2017, while North Korea's was US$1,700 in 2015. See Index Mundi website.

[13] Kim Il-sung, "Theses on Socialist Education", Published at the 14th Plenary

The North Korean leadership recognised the importance of science and technology in state building and national security as soon as Korea was liberated from Japanese colonial rule in 1945. The State Academy of Sciences was established in December 1952 to centralise and formalise the state's research and development efforts. The Academy is under the cabinet as a ministry-level institution responsible for national scientific research and development, including the area of computer science. In 1960, only seven years after the signing of the Korean War Armistice, North Korea assembled its first computer, the Chŏnjin-5500 (前進; advance), 13 years before its South Korean rival[14]. In 1970, an office or research center for general computer programming was established in the (State) Academy of Sciences to develop computer software[15]. Despite North Korea's earlier entry into the assembly of electronic devices and computers, Pyongyang has been unable to establish an independent ICT production base. Electronics and ICT components still account for a large portion of the country's imports[16].

By the late 1970s, North Korea incorporated science as one of the three pillars in its Second Seven-Year Economic Plan (1978-1984)[17]. While North Korean ideology emphasizes extreme nationalism and self-reliance, the regime has welcomed foreign technology transfers. For example, in 1977, Kim Il-sung told the KWP Central Committee, "As for science and technology from abroad, they should be taught from a Juche standpoint and adapted to the conditions and actual situation in our country"[18]. Two years later, North Korea expressed to the

---

Meeting of the Fifth Central Committee of the Workers' Party of Korea, 5 September 1977, Foreign Languages Publishing House, Pyongyang, Korea.

[14] 고경민, 북한의 *IT* 전략, Ko Kyŏng-min, *North Korea's IT Strategy*, Seoul, Communication Books, 2004, pp. 100-101.

[15] Ibid., pp. 106-107.

[16] 통일교육원, 2018 북한 이해 [Institute for Unification Education, 2018, *Understanding North Korea*], Seoul, December 2017, p. 130.

[17] The other two were *chuch'e* (self-reliant ideology) and modernisation. See Ko Kyŏng-min (2004), pp. 50-51.

[18] Kim Il-sung (1977).

outside world that it was interested developing an IT industry by seeking to build an integrated circuit plant under a project sponsored by the United Nations Development Program (UNDP) and the UN Industrial Development Organization (UNIDO)[19].

During the 1980s, Pyongyang established the foundation of its cyber networks and cyber capabilities. North Korea's IT sector reportedly received a boost in state support following Kim Il-sung's 1984 visit to East Germany, where he was impressed by German technology and computing[20]. North Korea opened its first computer assembly plant in 1983, and an electronic computation college in 1985[21]. The following year, North Korea established the Pyongyang Informatics Center (PIC) with support from the pro-North Korean General Association of Korean Residents in Japan and the UNDP[22]. The PIC was established with 10 staff members; now it has over 600[23]. Also in 1986, North Korea reportedly hired 25 Soviet instructors to train North Korean military students in "cyber warfare"[24].

When the Soviet Union and Eastern Bloc collapsed, North Korea suffered a terms of trade shock that preceded Kim Il-sung's

---

[19] P. Hayes, "DPRK Information Strategy - Does It Exist?" in A.Y. Mansourov (ed.), *Bytes and Bullets: Information Technology Revolution and National Security on the Korean Peninsula*, Honolulu, Asia-Pacific Center for Security Studies, 2005.

[20] Ko Kyŏng-min (2004), p. 89; H. Lee, J. Hwang, "ICT Development in North Korea: Changes and Challenges", *Information Technologies and International Development*, vol. 2, no. 1, Fall 2004, p. 77; M. Hallam, "North Korea cables reveal East Germany's deep-rooted suspicion of Kim regime", *Deutsche Welle*, 8 February 2018.

[21] P. Hayes (2005).

[22] Ibid.; P. Collins and F. Nixson, "Public sector management and the transition to a more open economy: Cautious reform in the Democratic People's Republic of Korea (DPRK)", *Public Administration and Development*, vol. 13, 1993, pp. 377-88.

[23] By 2003, the staff had grown to over 200. See 고경민, 북한의 IT 전략, Seoul, Communication Books, 2004, p. 108; http://nkinfo.unikorea.go.kr/nkp/overview/nkOverview.do?sumryMenuId=MENU_49.

[24] 윤규식, "북한의 사이버전 능력과 위협 전망," 군사논단, 제68호, 2011 년 겨울 [Yoon Kyu-sik, "The Prospects of North Korean Cyber War Capabilities and Threats", *Military Forum*, no. 68, Winter 2011].

death and succession in 1994, in addition to natural disasters and flooding that together sent the country into a famine and national crisis[25]. Despite extreme food insecurity during a period North Koreans call the "Arduous March," successor Kim Jong-il continued to emphasise ICT as an instrument to alleviate economic deprivation and to resolve national security challenges. In 1993, Kim Jong-il visited software research entities to stress the need to develop software programs. In 1996, Kim visited the [State] Academy of Sciences to emphasise the need to acquire foreign software technology; at the same time, he reportedly issued a directive to acquire foreign language journals and trade magazines for software development[26].

In 1995, when the effects of the famine were worsening, Kim Jong-il issued his directive to the Korean People's Army (KPA) General Staff to develop cyber warfare capabilities[27]. Kim reportedly told his generals, "In the Twentieth century, war is with bullets over oil. But in the Twenty-first century, war will be [fought as] information warfare"[28]. Kim reportedly issued a similar directive in 1998[29]. Of course, Kim's words would have rung hollow if North Korea did not have the institutions, infrastructure, and human resources to follow through.

---

[25] S. Haggard and M. Noland, "Hunger and Human Rights: The Politics of Famine in North Korea", US Committee for Human Rights in North Korea, 2005; S. Haggard, M. Noland, *Famine in North Korea: Markets, Aid, and Reform*, New York, Columbia University Press, 2009; H. Smith, *Hungry for Peace*, Washington D.C., USIP, 2005; A.S. Natsios, *The Great North Korean Famine: Famine, Politics, and Foreign Policy*, Washington D.C., USIP, 2001.

[26] Ko Kyŏng-min (2004), p. 105.

[27] The KPA was already studying the effects of "electronic intelligence warfare" in the first Persian Gulf War. The KPA also studied electronic warfare and cyber warfare doctrines developed by China's People's Liberation Army (PLA) in the 1990s. See Yoon Kyu-sik, (2011). 윤규식, "북한의 사이버전 능력과 위협 전망," 군사논단, 제68호, 2011 년 겨울

[28] Ibid.

[29] 김흥광, "북한의 사이버테러정보전 능력과 사이버보안대책 제언," NK지식인연대, 2009 [Kim Hŭng-gwang, "North Korea's Cyberterror and Information Warfare Capabilities: A Proposal for Cybersecurity Countermeasures", North Korea Intellectuals Solidarity, 2009].

During the 1990s, North Korea invested in a fiber-optic network with support from the UNDP after concluding a cooperative agreement in August 1990[30]. The agreement included support for the construction of the Pyongyang Fiber-Optic Cable Factory, which was completed in April 1992. The plant provided fiber-optic cable in the project to connect government offices, educational and research institutions, and military bases throughout the country[31]. The second stage of the project was completed in March 2000[32]. In the early 1990s, the [State] Academy of Sciences and Kim Il-sung University established a local area network (LAN) with a few other institutions[33]. In 1996, the UNDP office in Pyongyang established the first known Internet connection with the outside world[34]. At the same time, North Korea began working on *Kwangmyŏng*, the national intranet that commenced initial services in June 1997[35]. North Korea has exercised extreme control over Internet access, making the country the least connected in the world[36]. North Korea's Central Information Agency of Science and Technology (CIAST) hosts the servers for *Kwangmyŏng* and acts as a censor

[30] Ko Kyŏng-min (2004), pp. 98-100.

[31] A. Mansourov, *North Korea's Cyber Warfare and Challenges for the U.S.-ROK Alliance*, Academic Paper Series, Korea Economic Institute of America, 2 December 2014, p. 2; 임종인, 권유중, 장규현, 백승 조, "북한의 사이버전력 현황과 한국의 국가적 대응전략," 국방정책연구, 제29 권, 제4호, 2013 겨울, p. 21 [Im Jong-in, Kwŏn Yu-jung, Chang Gyu-hyŏn, Paek Sŭng-jo, "The Current Status of North Korea's Cyberwar Power, and South Korea's National Counter-Strategy", *The Quarterly Journal of Defense Policy Studies*, vol. 29, no. 4, winter 2013]; and J.S. Bermudez Jr, "SIGINT, EW, and EIW in the Korean People's Army: An Overview of Development and Organization," in AY. Mansourov (2005), pp. 244-45.

[32] Ko Kyŏng-min (2004), pp. 98-100.

[33] Ibid., p. 115.

[34] A. Mansourov (2014).

[35] J.S. Bermudez Jr. (2005), p. 245; Ko Kyŏng-min (2004), p. 115.

[36] North Korea is not even listed on most global indexes. For a brief look at North Korean Internet usage, see A. Martin, "This analysis of North Korean internet usage is a fascinating glimpse at the behaviour of the country's elite", *Alphr*, 25 July 2017.

and gatekeeper for content that it mines from the World Wide Web. CIAST was established in August 1963[37], so it has a long history of managing data and information for dissemination within the country. However, North Korea's responsibility for global Internet access, monitoring, and management could soon shift to the Pyongyang Internet Communication Bureau. Construction of the bureau's headquarters, which began in November 2015, is nearly complete, but its exact role and functions remain to be seen[38].

A main pillar of Pyongyang's ICT software and development capacity has been the Korea Computer Center (KCC), which was established in October 1990. The KCC was expanded in 1999 when it merged with the Ŭnbyŏl Computer Technology Research Institute, a software development center that had been established in 1995.[39] The KCC produces software and conducts research in the areas of artificial intelligence, fuzzy logic, image and video processing, text recognition, and machine translations, among others.[40] The KCC has subordinate research divisions focusing on operating systems, artificial intelligence, and information systems[41].

Human resources are the most important element for the development of science and technology, and for the sustainability of complex state projects. North Korea, a relative weakling in the international system, is a very strong state in terms of state-society relations and domestic governance[42]. North Korea

---

[37] Ko Kyŏng-min (2004), p. 117.

[38] M. Williams, "North Korea and the Internet: Building for the Future", North Korea Tech, 1 August 2018; "北, 평양 인터넷통신국 착공…'사회주의 건설에 중요'," ["http://newfocus.co.kr/client/news/viw.asp?ctcd=C01&mcate=M1001&nNewsNumb=20151117516" The North Breaks Ground on the Pyongyang Internet Communication Bureau… 'Important for Building Socialism'], *New Focus*, 27 November 2015.

[39] Ko Kyŏng-min (2004), pp. 109-112; http://nkinfo.unikorea.go.kr/nkp/overview/nkOverview.do?sumryMenuId=MENU_49.

[40] Ibid, p. 109.

[41] http://nkinfo.unikorea.go.kr/nkp/overview/nkOverviewdo?sumryMenuId=MENU_49.

[42] For a general review of state power in communist systems, see J. Kornai,

is the quintessential totalitarian state with a penetration of social control that Mussolini could only dream about. The state is able to select young students for special training in ICT and steer elite students into country's best schools.

Primary school students are introduced to ICT and computers in 4th and 5th grade, and ICT is part of the middle school and high school curriculums[43]. However, special No. 1 Middle Schools focus on science and technology for the country's best students, who must also come from politically loyal backgrounds. The first No. 1 Middle School was established in Pyongyang in 1984 under the directions of Kim Jong-il. By 1999, similar schools were established in each city, county, and district throughout the country to identify and educate the best science and technology students[44].

The premier North Korean institution of higher education is Kim Il-sung University, founded on 1 October 1946[45], before the establishment of the KPA (8 February 1948), the Democratic People's Republic of Korea (DPRK) (9 September 1948), and the ruling Korean Workers Party (30 June 1949). The university's College of Computer Science, established as the Faculty of Automation in 1977 and later renamed in 1997 and promoted to a college in 1999, conducts research and provides education in network systems, systems management and security, hardware, software, operating systems, sound and character recognition, information processing, and artificial intelligence[46].

Kim Chaek University of Technology (KUT), established in September 1948[47]. is considered the country's second top school in the fields of science and technology. The university

---

*The Socialist System: The Political Economy of Communism*, Princeton, Princeton University Press, 1992, pp. 33-48.

[43] 통일부 통일교육원, 2018 북한 이해 [Institute for Unification Education, 2018 Understanding North Korea], Seoul, December 2017, pp. 174-79.

[44] Ibid., p. 173.

[45] "Brief history of Kim Il Sung University", Kim Il-sung University.

[46] "College of Computer Science", Kim Il-sung University; http://nkinfo.unikorea.go.kr/nkp/overview/nkOverview.do?sumryMenuId=MENU_49.

[47] "History", Kim Chaek University of Technology.

has a number of colleges, departments, and institutes covering the full spectrum of ICT[48]. Including:

- College of Mechanical Science and Technology
- College of Information Science and Technology
- Faculty of Resources Probing Engineering
- Faculty of Electrical Engineering
- Faculty of Electronics
- Faculty of Automation Engineering
- Faculty of Communications
- Faculty of Applied Mathematics
- Nano Physics Engineering Institute
- Robotics Institute
- Semiconductor Institute
- IT Institute
- Analytic Instrument Institute
- Electric Power System Institute
- Electric Engineering Institute
- Information Communication Institute

The graduate school provides degrees[49] in several ICT related fields:

- Machine-building Engineering
- Mechanical Engineering
- Aeronautical Engineering
- Optical Engineering
- Computer Engineering
- Information Processing
- Resources Probing Engineering
- Mining Engineering
- Metal Engineering
- Material Engineering
- Heat Engineering
- Electrical Engineering

---

48 "Structure", Kim Chaek University of Technology.

49 "Postgraduate", Kim Chaek University of Technology.

- Electronics
- Science of Communications
- Automation Engineering
- Applied Mathematics
- Physics
- Applied Chemistry

In 2001, KUT and Syracuse University in the U.S. began a scientific engagement process in the area of ICT[50]. The following year, the two universities began a joint project for KUT to establish North Korea's first electronic library[51]. In February 2010, KUT opened its Online College for distance learning. The school boasts 24,000 online students and reports the number has been increasing every year[52]. The total KUT enrollment on campus reportedly is 12,500 with about 10% of them majoring in computer science[53].

Pyongyang Computer Technology College was established in 1985 as the Pyongyang Electronic Computation College before adopting its current name in December 1999. The school has a student body of about 2,500 and a faculty and staff of about 200[54]. Other important North Korean educational institutions for ICT education and training are the Kim Il-sung Military Academy, the Kim Il Military Academy, the Pyongyang National Defense College, and the Ryongsŏng Light Electrical Engineering College[55].

---

[50] H. Seo and S. Thorson, "Academic Science Engagement with North Korea", Korea Economic Institute of America Academic Paper Series on Korea, vol. 3, pp. 105-121; S.J. Thorson, "Universities and Networks: Scientific Engagement with North Korea", *Science & Diplomacy*, vol. 1, no. 2, June 2012.

[51] http://nkinfo.unikorea.go.kr/nkp/overview/nkOverview.do?sumryMenuId=MENU_49.

[52] "Distance Education", Kim Chaek University of Technology.

[53] Ko Kyŏng-min (2004), p. 114; http://nkinfo.unikorea.go.kr/nkp/overview/nkOverview.do?sumryMenuId=MENU_49.

[54] "평양콤퓨터기술대학", Encyclopedia of Korean Culture, The Academy of Korean Studies; Ko Kyŏng-min (2004), pp. 114-115.

[55] D.A. Pinkston, "Inter-Korean Rivalry in the Cyber Domain: The North Korean

## Control and Utilisation of North Korean Cyber Capacity

Over the past three and a half decades, North Korea developed the institutional and human resources to establish a significant capacity for benign or positive activities, as well as disruptive or damaging actions. North Korea's cyber capacity is remarkable given the country's repressive political and social control. There is no private ICT sector, no civil society, and access to the global Internet is restricted to a very small number or regime elites. The regime maintains a repressive system of monitoring and surveillance that contradicts the ideals upon which the Internet was established: openness, decentralisation, freedom of expression, and democratic participation. North Korea's domestic politics, internal governance, and state objectives determine how Pyongyang uses its instruments of state power – just like other states. But North Korea's historical past, ideology, politics, and institutional design have led to a sui generis case of national entry into cyberspace.

The DPRK (or North Korea) is an authoritarian one-party state established in September 1948, and now under the third generation of Kim family rule[56]. According to its constitution, the DPRK is a socialist state based on the ideology and leadership exploits of Kim Il-sung and Kim Jong-il. Under the official narrative, the ideology and leadership of the Kims constitute a fundamental national asset that guarantees the DPRK's prosperity. The constitution requires all state activities be performed under the guidance of the Korean Workers Party (KWP)[57]. However, the KWP is proclaimed to be the "party of

Cyber Threat in the Sŏn'gun Era", *Georgetown Journal of International Affairs*, vol. 17, no. 3, Fall/Winter 2016, pp. 60-76.

[56] For background on the establishment of North Korea's authoritarian system, see D.A. Pinkston, "Kimism in Sŏn'gun Korea: The Third Generation of the Kim Dynasty", in B. Howe (ed.) *National Security, State-Centricity, and Governance in East Asia*, Palgrave MacMillan, 2018.

[57] Article 11, DPRK Socialist Constitution (2013).

Kim Il-sung," making the political system extremely centralised and personalistic even when compared to the classical communist systems of the XX century[58].

Nominally, the KWP Party Congress holds all decision-making authority for the Party. When the Party Congress is not meeting, that authority is held by the Central Committee (CC)[59]. However, in practice special functional committees deliberate and decide policy in the shadow of democratic-centralism and the dictatorship of the proletariat. The politburo decides overall party policy, and the five-member standing committee can act on behalf of the full politburo. The 14-member Central Military Committee (CMC) decides military policy, and the CC functional departments direct ICT-related policy as applicable. The Organization and Guidance Department (OGD) maintains personnel files of all party members and monitors their loyalty, which is critical in maintaining party discipline and internal security.

The CC Science and Education Department oversees science and technology education, including the curriculum and guidelines for ICT education throughout the school system. The state and the cabinet execute the production plans for the supply of ICT hardware. The cabinet is led by Premier Pak Pong-ju, who also serves on the Politburo Standing Committee and on the CMC. Pak is supported by nine vice-premiers who oversee the State Science and Technology Committee (a cabinet-level entity), the Ministry of Machine Industry, and the Ministry of Electronic Industry. Finally, the State Academy of Sciences is nominally under the cabinet as well.

North Korea has a wide range of cyber capabilities. Some of them probably have not been deployed since once cyber tools have been released into cyberspace, their characteristics can be

[58] Important aspects of these systems include a one-party state, democratic-centralism, an intrusive state that seeks to control all economic transactions and social relationships. For example, see J. Kornai (1992).

[59] The Seventh Party Congress was held in May 2016, but the Sixth Party Congress was held in October 1980.

analysed, and countermeasures can be applied to neutralise their effects. North Korea has demonstrated the following capabilities:

- Computer network attack (CNA)
- Computer network exploitation (CNE)
- Computer network defence (CND)
- Influence operations
- Cyber crime
- Cyber terrorism

Although North Korea has not demonstrated the capability to create cyber (physical) weapons with kinetic effects (such as Stuxnet), the country has the human resources and understanding of programmable logic controllers (PLC) and supervisory control and data acquisition systems (SCADA) software. Therefore, the creation and deployment of malware to damage power grids, dams, gas pipelines, and other industrial control systems is not beyond North Korea's capabilities. Analysts were concerned that Pyongyang could employ such an attack following a North Korean-attributed cyberattack against [South] Korea Hydro and Nuclear Power (KHNP) in December 2014. The breach occurred when employees became victims of phishing emails with malware that exfiltrated blueprints of a nuclear reactor, data on power plant support systems, and personal data from over 10,000 KHNP employees[60].

## Execution and Control of Cyber Operations

All military and state institutions in North Korea carry out their missions under the guidance of the KWP. This also applies to cyber operations, which are split between the General Staff of the KPA and the Reconnaissance General Bureau (RGB). In peacetime, the General Staff is subordinated to the Ministry of the People's Armed, but in wartime the General Staff reports

[60] J.S. Kwaak, "North Korea Blamed for Nuclear-Power Plant Hack", *The Wall Street Journal*, 17 March 2015.

directly to the KPA supreme commander (Kim Jong-un).

The General Staff's Electronic Warfare Department (also known as the Command Automation Department) is tasked with electronic warfare operations and military communications. The Department's Office 31 reportedly develops hacking tools, Office 32 reportedly develops military-related software, and Office 56 reportedly develops software for command and control communications. According to South Korean reports, each of these offices has about 50-60 military officers. Office 204, also under the General Staff, targets the South Korean military with phishing emails[61].

The RGB was established around February 2009 when the KPA's Reconnaissance Bureau was merged with the KWP's Operations Department and Office 35. The new RGB was placed under direct control of the National Defense Commission, which was replaced by the State Affairs Commission in the 2016 constitutional revision. Nevertheless, the RGB reported directly to the chairman, who was Kim Jong-il and now is Kim Jong-un. The reorganised RGB was given greater powers to conduct intelligence, espionage, special operations, and computer network operations, particularly regarding the South[62].

The RGB reportedly has six departments:

- First Department (also known as the "Operations Department," and formerly the KWP Operations Department)
- Second Department (also known as the "Reconnaissance Department," and formerly the reconnaissance Department under the KPA General Staff)

---

[61] 정재욱, " '남한의 선거에 개입' 지시한 김정은", 미래한국, 2016년 3월 22일 [Chŏng Jae-uk, "Interference in South Korean Election Directed by Kim Jong-un", *Future Korea*, 22 March 2016].

[62] 김윤영, "북한 대남공작기관 실체와 대남공작 변화," 북한연구소, 2017년 3월 22일, [Kim Yun-yŏng, "The Reality of North Korea's Agency for Operations against the South, and Changes in Operations against the South", North Korea Research Institute, 22 March 2017]; J.S. Bermudez Jr, *A New Emphasis on Operations against South Korea?*, 38 North, Special Report no. 4, 11 June 2010.

- Third Department (also known as the "Technical Reconnaissance Department")
- Fifth Department (also known as the "Foreign Intelligence Department," and formerly the KWP's Office 35)
- Sixth Department (responsible for military policies towards the South and North-South mil-mil dialog)
- Seventh Department (logistical and rear support)[63]

The Third Department is either also known as the "110 Institute" or "Lab 110", or the 110 Institute is part of the RGB's Third Department. Less than a month after the cyberattack against Sony Pictures Entertainment became public, the United States sanctioned the RGB for the attack[64]. Lab 110 also was named in a criminal complaint field in a US District Federal Court on 8 June 2018. The complaint filed by the FBI in Central District of California alleged that Mr. Park Jin-hyok violated the US criminal code to commit conspiracy and conspiracy to commit wire fraud[65]. The complaint is the result of an FBI investigation that took years and that provides insights into the methods and practices of North Korean malicious cyber actors, which will be elaborated below.

The relationship between the KPA General Staff, the RGB, and the civilian educational institutions mentioned in the previous section is sketchy. While schools and universities provide the general human resources for the KPA and RGB, the extent of collaboration in the development of malware and hacking tools is uncertain. However, the leadership's sensitivity to state

---

[63] 김윤영, "북한 대남공작기관 실체와 대남공작 변화,"북한연구소, 2017년 3월 22일 [Kim Yun-yŏng, "The Reality of North Korea's...", cit.].

[64] "Treasury Imposes Sanctions Against the Government of The Democratic People's Republic Of Korea", US Department of the Treasury Press Release, 2 January 2015.

[65] "United States of America v. PARK JIN HYOK, also known as ('aka') 'Jin Hyok-park,' aka 'Pak Jin-hek,' Defendant", Criminal Case Number MJ 18-1479, filed in the United States District Court for Central District of California by Nathan P. Shields, Special Agent, FBI, 8 June 2018.

security means that, in general, operations security is strict; projects and programs are compartmentalised. While collaboration across military and civilian entities is probably low, there are multiple cyber tools available on the Internet, and the senior leadership can issue directives for inter-agency cooperation when necessary.

Since cyber tools for CNE and CNA are similar, intent usually determines outcomes once an intruder infiltrates a network. The party exercises strict control of the state, the economy, society, the media, and cyberspace in North Korea. Civil society is non-existent. North Korean activities in cyberspace are in accordance with Party guidance and directives. Inter-Korean relations and regional geopolitics will continue to influence North Korea and how the leadership crafts its Internet policy and utilises its cyber capabilities. Paradoxically, past inter-Korean cooperation could have produced unintended and unanticipated consequences by inadvertently helping North Korea build its cyber capacity.

## Chosun Expo Joint Venture, Korea Expo Joint Venture, the GOP, the Lazarus Group, and APT38

Attribution problems in cyberspace are well known, especially when actors make efforts to conceal their true identities. Analysing cyberattacks can take months or years, and investigations are not always conclusive. However, North Korea's persistent and brazen cyber activities have left sufficient evidence to expose the actors, their capabilities, and motivations. Private IT security firms have analysed past cyberattacks, and they have assigned the culprits fictitious pseudonyms such as the Lazarus Group[66] and APT38[67] (Advanced Persistent Threat 38). The firms could be motivated for legal reasons or for plausible

[66] Novetta, "Operation Blockbuster: Unraveling the Long Thread of the Sony Attack", February 2016.

[67] FireEye, "APT38: Un-usual Suspects", 3 October 2018.

deniability to avoid possible retribution from North Korea. For what it's worth, the perpetrators of the SPE hacking claimed to be the "Guardians of Peace" or "GOP," probably in an effort to deceive people into believing that the hackers were a non-state criminal organisation.

As mentioned above, the capabilities and tools for CNE and CNA are similar. Once skilled hackers penetrate computer networks, their next actions usually depend upon their motivations and objectives. Therefore, inter-Korean reconciliation should be expected to mitigate malevolent cyber activity by North Korean hackers since the KWP and the state exercise tight control. If the KWP is interested in better inter-Korean ties, the Party should be expected to restrain North Korean ICT institutions from taking actions that could undermine those interests. From the South Korean perspective, steering North Korean computer specialists towards legitimate ICT activities and business pursuits is another way to reduce North Korean motivations for engaging in cybercrime.

That was the context behind North-South ICT cooperation that began in the wake of the first inter-Korean summit in June 2000. Three months prior to the summit, South Korea's Samsung and North Korea's KCC established a joint software development enterprise in Beijing[68]. After the summit, subsequent talks and agreements surrounding ICT cooperation influenced the development of North Korea's cyber capacity, which inadvertently could have helped foster the emergence of North Korean hackers. In 2001, a South Korean delegation visited Pyongyang for four rounds of talks on ICT cooperation in February, March, April, and July. During the fourth visit in July, the two sides established a "Unification IT Forum", and delivered some IT materials and manuals[69].

In May 2001, South Korea's Ministry of Unification (MOU) approved a license for South Korean firms Hana Biz and NTrack

[68] Ko Kyŏng-min (2004), p. 203; Yoo Hyang Kim, "North Korea's Cyberpath," *Asian Perspective*, vol. 28, no. 3, 2004, pp. 191-209.
[69] Ko Kyŏng-min (2004), p. 200.

to establish a joint venture in Dandong, China with the North Korean "People's Economic Cooperation Association" and the Pyongyang Informatics Center (PIC). Hana Biz provided US$2 million in capital investment for the Hana Program Center joint venture, and North Korea provided the manpower to develop software[70]. The idea was to integrate South Korean capital and international market access with low-cost and highly skilled North Korean ICT labour. The project was typical of the objectives outlined by Kim Dae-jung's Sunshine Policy of engagement with the North to increase economic interdependence, reconciliation, and eventual Korean unification. For North Korea, inter-Korean cooperation in ICT presented an opportunity for technology transfers and adopting know-how from a more advanced ICT partner who could facilitate that process without foreign language barriers. Furthermore, North Korea sought capital investment and access to international markets through South Korean partners[71]. By the end of 2001, the MOU approved five inter-Korean economic cooperation projects; four of them were for the joint development of software[72].

By August 2002, there were six joint IT joint projects in operation with about US$9 million in investment provided by South Korean firms[73]. One of these joint ventures was formed by South Korea's Hoonnet, North Korea's Korea Jangsaeng Trading Corporation[74], and the Pan-Pacific Economic

[70] Ibid., p. 200.; "중국 단동, 남북합작 정보기술회사 하나프로그램센터 출범[정경수]", 10 May 2001 [North-South IT Joint Venture Company Hana Program Center Launched in Dandong, China [Chŏng Kyŏng-su]], 10 May 2001; "(주)하나비즈닷컴, (주)앤드랙 남북협력사업자 승인," 통일신문, 7 May 2001, http://m.unityinfo.co.kr/289 [North-South Cooperative Venture Approved for Hana Biz.com (Inc.) and NTrack (Inc.)"], Tongil Shinmun, 7 May 2001.

[71] T. Beal, "E-Unification of Koreas: Dreams, Plans and Realities", in A.Y. Mansourov (2005).

[72] Ko Kyŏng-min (2004), p. 204.

[73] Ibid., p. 205.

[74] "Korea Jangsaeng Trading Corporation", Narnara website, 26 March 2014, "조

Development Association of Korean Nationals (PPEDAKN)[75]. The Association, based in Beijing, is "a semi-governmental organisation focused on economic exchange and attracting international investment to North Korea"[76]. The new firm was named Korea Lotto Joint Venture[77]. North Korea's Jangsaeng Trading Corporation held a 51% share, and Hoonnet held 30%. The PPEDAKN and other investors held 19%[78].

Korea Lotto Joint Venture established the first websites hosted by a server in North Korea. The websites (www.dklotto.com; www.jupae.com; and www.mybaduk.com) were designed for a lottery, online casino, and paduk (go) gaming[79]. The joint venture also aimed to provide an internet sales outlet for North Korean products. The websites went online in April 2002, but the project immediately ran into problems. The president of Honnet, Kim Bŏm-hun, and three employees were detained in Pyongyang when they were accused of violating the terms of the joint venture agreement. Kim then had trouble with South Korea's MOU for having violated the terms of the license. The dispute centered on North Korea's insistence on running a gambling website, while the South Korean government had believed the gaming website would only be for game tokens or points and not real money. When the gambling website began to attract large numbers of South Koreans, it drew the attention of the South Korean government, and MOU withdrew the license[80].

---

선장생무역회사" , Narnara website, 26 March 2014.

[75] T. Beal (2005); F. Librero and P.B. Arinto (eds.), *Digital Review of Asia Pacific 2007–2008*, Saga, Orbicom, International Development Research Centre (IDRC), 7 January 2008, p. 248.

[76] M. Williams, "North Korea to exhibit domestic software in Beijing", *ITWorld Canada*, 17 February 2002.

[77] The Korean name is longer and could be directly translated as "[North] Korean Internet Lottery and Programming Development Joint Venture".

[78] Ko Kyŏng-min (2004), p. 252; Ko Soo-suk, "North Korea hopes to cash in on interest in Internet lotto", *Korea Joongang Daily*, 22 March 2002.

[79] Ko Kyŏng-min (2004), p. 252.

[80] Sang-Hun Choe, "Online gambling via N. Korea leading to a web of trouble",

After Hoonnet had to withdraw from the project, the North Korean partner ran the project independently, providing goods and services, including software development and gambling[81]. The North Korean entity later changed its name to Chosun Expo, and changed its website to http://www.chosunexpo.com, and its domain remained registered to Korea Lotto Joint Venture[82]. While Chosun Expo engages in legitimate business projects, at some point, Chosun Expo staff, possibly in cooperation with other North Korean entities, began executing cybercrimes. According to the FBI criminal complaint filed in June 2018, the evidence indicates that "Park Jin-hyok, a graduate of Kim Chaek University of Technology, began working with the Korea Expo Joint Venture in 2002 as an online game developer"[83].

The FBI criminal complaint filed against Park is a detailed report outlining the methods that Park (and likely associates) allegedly used to commit CNE, CNA, and wire fraud against Sony Pictures Entertainment, the Bangladesh Central Bank, US defence contractor Lockheed Martin, UK production company Mammoth Screen, and AMC Theaters in the United States[84]. The FBI alleges that Chosun Expo is a "North Korean government front company for [the RGB's] Lab 110"[85]. FBI forensic analysis linked Internet activity behind the attacks to North Korean IP addresses, and the use of social media to conduct research and reconnaissance on phishing and hacking targets. Proxies, hop points from compromised computers, email

---

*The Las Vegas Sun*, 26 January 2004; 이상헌, "'훈넷' 남북경협사업자 승인취소 [통일부]," *매일경제신문*, 19 January 2004, http://news.mk.co.kr/newsRead.php?sc=30000001&year=2004&no=19290.

[81] "United States of America v. PARK JIN HYOK, also known as ('aka') 'Jin Hyok Park,' aka 'Pak Jin Hek,' Defendant"…, cit., p. 136.

[82] "Chosun Expo", NK Tech website, last updated on 16 February 2011.

[83] "United States of America v. PARK JIN HYOK, also known as ('aka') 'Jin Hyok Park,' aka 'Pak Jin Hek,' Defendant"…, cit., p. 143.

[84] "United States of America v. PARK JIN HYOK, also known as ('aka') 'Jin Hyok Park,' aka 'Pak Jin Hek,' Defendant"…, cit.

[85] Ibid.

address books, and recovery email addresses provided for Chosun Expo linked accounts combine to show that North Korea was behind these cyberattacks, as well as the creation and release of the WannaCry ransomware in 2017[86].

Independent analysis by cybersecurity firms such as FireEye and Group I-B have traced the theft of $81 million from the Bangladeshi Central Bank, as well as similar attempts to steal hundreds of millions of dollars from the Vietnam TP Bank, the Far Eastern International Bank in Taiwan, Mexico's Bancomext, and Banco de Chile by hacking into the SWIFT system and executing illicit bank transfers[87]. FireEye assesses that two separate North Korean groups are engaged in hacking activities, claiming that "APT38's primary mission is targeting financial institutions and manipulating inter-bank financial systems to raise large sums of money for the North Korean regime"[88].

While other activities such as cyber espionage might be managed by another North Korean entity or firm, in some respects it doesn't matter because all such activities must be executed under the guidance and authority of the KWP. CNE, CNA and other cyber activities could be delegated under a division of labour for efficiency purposes, or for security and redundancy reasons. Different organisations can develop expertise through specialisation, but security and control are paramount for the regime. Hence, the leadership would extend oversight and monitoring to its cyber institutions just as it does throughout the rest of the state, military, and society. Given the complexity of IT, the knowledge required to monitor activities, and the asymmetric information problems for the senior leadership that lacks IT expertise, the KWP has a need and strong incentive to institutional redundancy in ICT to ensure that North Korea's IT specialists do not stray from party guidance. Of course, monitoring is costly and imperfect, but the risk for IT agents

---

[86] Ibid.

[87] FireEye, "APT38: Un-usual Suspects", 3 October 2018; Group I-B, "Lazarus arisen: architecture, tools, attribution", 30 May 2017.

[88] FireEye (2018), p. 6.

engaging in exploitative behaviour for personal is high. In most cases, most of the time, North Korean IT personnel should-be expected to be acting in accordance with KWP and state directives.

FireEye's recent report tracks the financial pressures as a result of increasingly strict economic and financial sanctions against North Korea, and North Korean cybercrimes to acquire hard currency. Financial institutions have an incentive to cover up computer network breaches and cyber theft since it could expose them to legal liability and undermine confidence and market value. Nevertheless, banks reportedly have been targeted for cyber theft, most likely by North Korean hackers, in North America, South America, Europe, Asia, and Africa. The attempted bank heists have totalled over US$1 billion[89]. In January 2018, hackers tried to steal US$110 million from Bancomext through the SWIFT system but failed. Subsequently, they were able to take about US$15 million from Mexico's domestic money transfer system. In late May, hackers stole about $10 million from Banco de Chile and wiped the master boot records (MBRs) of about 9,000 computers and servers[90]. While it is too early to attribute the attacks to North Korea with absolute certainty, these attacks are consistent with North Korea's previous malicious cyber activities. North Korea has demonstrated the capability to execute the attacks, and the demand for hard currency is evident. Furthermore, the magnitude and scale of these operations make it virtually impossible for rogue North Korean agents to execute these attacks in violation of guidance or directives from the top. This has become a severe global problem requiring international cooperation, but with no easy solutions. North Korea has a long history of illicit activities including drug smuggling, counterfeiting, and nuclear proliferation. So far, cybercrime offers remote access to

---

[89] "United States of America v. PARK JIN HYOK, also known as ('aka') 'Jin Hyok-park,' aka 'Pak Jin-hek,' Defendant"…, cit.

[90] G. Burton, "Banco de Chile falls victim to SWIFT money transfer hack that crashed 9,000 computers and 500 servers", *Computing*, 11 June 2018.

illicit revenue without the risks of being detained and prosecuted abroad. The ultimate solution lies in North Korea's reform, transformation, and integration into the international community whereby it will abide by international law and norms. However, this could take a long time.

## Conflict or Cooperation on the Korean Peninsula?

North Korea's foreign policy and national defence policy, as well as the way North Korea uses its ICT (information, communications, and technology) resources in the context of these policy realms, are closely tethered to national division and relations with the South. After suffering 35 years of Japanese colonial rule, Korea was finally liberated as the Japanese empire collapsed. However, Korea has remained divided since the end of the war. During the colonial period, Korean nationalists were divided by ideology – some seeking liberation through Marxism-Leninism while others espoused the ideals of liberal-democracy and the Wilsonian "right to self-determination". The gap widened since Korea sat on a fault line of the emerging Cold War. In August 1945, Moscow and Washington agreed to accept the Japanese surrender of military forces in a northern and southern sector divided by the 38th parallel. After three years of wrangling, the two sides failed to agree upon the terms for a unified government, so two separate states were formed. Enmity besieged the peninsula and has lingered there since the fratricidal war (1950-1953).

The conflict ended in an armistice – a ceasefire signed by the commanders of the Chinese People's Volunteers, the Korean People's Army, and the United Nations Command. For 70 years, the two Koreas have been locked in a zero-sum game where the DPRK and the Republic of Korea (ROK) claim to be the sole legitimate government for all the Korean people and territory. Both governments are committed to national unification. North Korea tried to unify the peninsula by force and failed, but Pyongyang has committed limited armed attacks and aggressive actions including sinking ships and capturing fishing vessels, shooting down aircraft, dispatching guerillas into the South to "trigger a people's uprising", and sending special forces into Seoul in a raid to assassinate the president[91].

Although the two sides have dodged some close calls and avoided a suspension of the armistice and a return to wartime conditions, there have been periods of thaws and near reconciliation. The signatories of the armistice recommended that a political conference of the two sides meet within three months "to settle through negotiation the questions of the withdrawal of all foreign forces from Korea, the peaceful settlement of the Korean question, etc". The conference didn't happen, and there have only been sporadic political dialogs.

The Cold War structure was relatively stable even though Korea was right on the fault line. The alliance structure, militarisation of the peninsula, and nuclear weapons created a stability-instability paradox that arguably enabled or permitted the periodic military skirmishes aimed at coercion, testing resolve, or demonstrating strength by the leadership to consolidate authority in Pyongyang. However, at times of international geopolitical shifts, the two Koreas engaged in political dialogue, at least in part to manage uncertainty. In 1972, the two Koreas issued their July 4th Communiqué in the wake of Nixon's Guam Doctrine and rapprochement with China. Seoul and Pyongyang repeated the process in 1991 with high-level talks and the signing of inter-Korean agreements as the Cold War was ending. However, the cycle stalled through the 1990s until being revived under Kim Dae-jung's "sunshine policy".

Despite efforts at reconciliation and several inter-Korean agreements, true reconciliation and peaceful coexistence has been elusive. Critics of North Korea argue that "peace offensives" are tactical measures to support the strategic objectives of "completing the revolution, achieving the final victory, and

---

[91] For a chronology of North Korean belligerent actions from 1950 until 2007, see Congressional Research Service, "North Korean Provocative Actions, 1950-2007", CRS Report for Congress, Order Code RL30004, 20 April 2007.

liberating the South". The North Korean leadership is rational and wishes to survive. Mutual deterrence is robust, but misperception or miscalculation are always possible. North Korea has been blamed for several cyber operations including information exfiltration and data theft (espionage), cybercrime and vandalism, and information operations to influence public opinion in the South.

The Party exerts tight control – but not absolute control – over cyber assets and personnel. Nevertheless, North Korean hackers or cyber warriors are elite members of North Korean society and are rewarded accordingly. Some have travelled abroad to conduct operations in China and Southeast Asia. Deviating from party guidance would endanger or terminate their privileged access to the Internet, a high price to pay in a country where generally one does not get second chances after disobeying the party.

Engagement and détente are likely to reduce the occurrence of malicious North Korean cyberattacks, but until North Korea escapes from economic sanctions, the regime will face pressures to acquire funds through cybercrime and other means. Pyongyang should be expected to continue cyber espionage since there are really no disincentives to cease CNE for intelligence collection. While frowned upon and considered a violation of sovereignty, states have not sought legal recourse when a target of espionage. States appear to be acquiescing to an emerging norm of accepting cyber espionage for national security objectives, although the trajectory for cases of state-sponsored and non-state industrial espionage is less certain.

As long as the two Koreas remain locked in a zero-sum rivalry for legitimacy, and as long as North Korea remains a family dictatorship under the KWP, Pyongyang is very likely to maintain the political objectives of "completing the revolution, achieving the final victory, and liberating the South". That means acting opportunistically to undermine confidence in the South Korean government, economy, and society. In the case of renewed military conflict, North Korea would seek to prevent intervention by the US and other South Korean allies. In sum, Pyongyang could use cyber means to undermine political support in the sending states that provided support to the South under the United Nations Command during the Korean War. In the case of conflict in Korea, the North would likely use cyber warfare as a force multiplier by creating chaos and paralysing computer networks in the South. However, to prevent rapid intervention by allies, physical geography is irrelevant for North Korean CNO. Japan, which hosts a number of US military support bases, could be targeted. Sending state allies such as Australia, Canada, the UK, France, New Zealand, and the Netherlands could be subject to cyberattacks to influence political support and resolve[92].

Private firms and governments have insufficient recourse in response to North Korean cyberattacks and threats. Common computer hygiene and security practices such as updated software and security patches, avoiding phishing scams, and using anti-virus software, can and should be supported. However, these practices are inadequate to avert persistent and sophisticated attacks from North Korean hackers. Deterrence in cyberspace is difficult. Timely and targeted punishment often is impossible. Clear attribution can take months or years, and the costs of detailed investigations are high. If perpetrators are identified, plaintiffs often cannot seek legal recourse because the accused are protected by their host nation. The US has indicted Russian hackers and Park Jin-hyok. Of course, it is extremely unlikely that Russia or North Korea will ever extradite them. In the case of North Korea, the Republic of Korea claims to be the sole legitimate government for all the Korean people and territory. According to the South Korean

[92] The 16 sending states that sent combat forces to support South Korea were Australia, Belgium, Canada, Colombia, Ethiopia, France, Greece, Luxembourg, the Netherlands, New Zealand, Philippines, South Africa, Thailand, Turkey, the United Kingdom, and the United States. Of course, these countries (except for the US) are not treaty bound to help defend South Korea. It would be a political decision depending on the situation and context.

constitution, the Korean people in the North are also ROK citizens and nominally should be held accountable under South Korean law. Firms and governments might consider filing legal claims in South Korean courts against suspected North Korean cyber criminals. It would have no immediate deterrent effect, and the current South Korean government probably would not welcome such action, viewing it as a hindrance to current efforts towards inter-Korean reconciliation. However, legal action in South Korean courts would create a foundation of facts, help signal resolve and seriousness in addressing North Korean cyber threats, and provide legal recourse in the case of future Korean unification.

# 5. Iran's Cybered Warfare Meets Western Cyber-Insecurity

Lior Tabansky

A security threat stems from a combination of intent and capability. According to the current National Security Strategy of the United States of America, Iranian expansion, jihadist ideology, and regional rivalries have for years convulsed the Middle East[1]. Iran exploits cyber technology for every instrument of power, but IT-security practitioners only focus on technical aspects of the adversarial action. Similarly, many political analysts fail to overcome conceptual limitations regarding state responsibility for cyberattacks. The article aims to strategically analyse cyber power, integrating strategic Iran's intent and Iran's latest global cyber offense. Improved conceptualisation of cyber power may mitigate the Western difficulties with providing national cybersecurity.

## Cyber Power

Kuehl has defined cyber power as "[...] the ability to use cyberspace to create advantages and influence events in other operational environments and across the instruments of power"[2]. Cyber power thus cuts across Diplomatic, Informational,

[1] National Security Strategy of the United States of America, December 2017.

[2] D.T. Kuehl, "Cyberspace and Cyberpower", in F.D. Kramer, S.H. Starr, and L.K. Wentz (eds.), *Cyberpower and National Security*, National Defense University Press, Potomac Books, 2009.

Military, and Economic (DIME) instruments of power as technology morphs and interconnects these elements. These changes enable numerous known and unknown methods to produce preferred outcomes within and outside cyberspace. Since most of the world's information is digitally produced, processed, stored, and transmitted, cyber power must be intertwined with information[3]. Indeed, adversaries have long experimented with applying cyber power in espionage-driven economic damage, threats to critical infrastructure, and mass subversion[4]. Joseph Samuel Nye, Jr, one of the most influential International Relations scholars as well as an experienced practitioner, defined hard and soft power in a seminal 1990 article[5]. Hard power relies on coercion and payment, while soft power uses the framing of agendas, attraction, or persuasion. Manipulation of information may, in principle, assist each type of hard and soft power along a spectrum from command to co-option. Two decades later, Nye also masterfully discussed cyber power, including both physical and informational aspects[6].

Cybered conflict, the term coined by Demchak and Dombrowski, means that adversarial and competitive relationships have a significant computerised dimension. The success or failure of major participants is critically dependent on computerised key activities along the path of events.

> Cybered conflict differs from cyber war or cyber battle. The latter is fully technological and could, in principle, be conducted entirely within a network. It is normally a component of the former. A cybered conflict is any conflict of national significance in which key events determining the path to the generally accepted outcome of the conflict could not have proceeded unless cyber means were non-substitutable and critically involved[7].

---

[3] J.S. Nye Jr, "Soft Power", *Foreign policy*, 1990.

[4] J. Healey and K. Grindal (eds.), *A Fierce Domain: Conflict in Cyberspace, 1986 to 2012*, Cyber Conflict Studies Association, 2013.

[5] J.S. Nye Jr, (1990).

[6] J.S. Nye Jr, *Cyber Power*, Belfer Center for Science and International Affairs, Harvard Kennedy School, 2010.

[7] C.C. Demchak and P. Dombrowski, "Rise of a Cybered Westphalian Age",

To illustrate the adversarial cybered operations and their role as an instrument of power, I analyse Iran's strategy, goals, and cyber means, employing the recently disclosed Iranian cyber offense campaign.

## Iran National Security Strategy and the Volatile Environment

The Islamic Republic of Iran is a revolutionary ideology-driven regime. Given the history of the 1979 revolution, the main threat to Iran is the US: Khamenei refers to the US as the "Great Satan", and to Israel as the "Little Satan". The risk of Western military invasion was high in Iran's eyes when the US invaded Iraq to topple Saddam's regime. It is no longer a viable option, but instead, Iran fears Western actions to topple Iran's regime from within. Ayatollah Khamenei calls this creeping infiltration of subversive foreign influences to undermine the social cohesion and legitimacy of the Islamic Republic "soft warfare".

The Internet and the World Wide Web promised a drastic blow to national information controls[8].Western proponents of "liberation technology"[9] and the US Presidents Reagan, Bush, Clinton, and Obama – all expressed a deep Western conviction

*Strategic Studies Quarterly*, Spring 2011, Ft. Belvoir, Air Univ Maxwell Afb Al Defense Technical Information Center, 2011. Fn.1; Chris C. Demchak, who introduced the term cybered conflict, is Grace M. Hopper Professor of Cyber Security in United States Naval War College.

[8] This fascinating issue exceeds the scope of the paper. For early criticism, see: E. Morozov, "Iran Elections: A Twitter Revolution?", *Washington Post*, 17 June 2009; E. Morozov, *The Net Delusion: The Dark Side of Internet Freedom*, New York, NY, Public Affairs, 2011.

[9] See K.A. Hill and J.E. Hughes, "Is the Internet an Instrument of Global Democratization?", *Democratization* vol. 6, no. 2, 1999; C. Weare, "The Internet and Democracy: The Causal Links between Technology and Policy", *International Journal of Public Administration* vol. 25, no. 5, 2002; R.J. Deibert and R. Rohozinski, "Liberation Vs. Control: The Future of Cyberspace", *Journal of Democracy*, vol. 21, no. 4, 2010, pp. 43-57; and L. Diamond, "Liberation Technology", *Journal of Democracy*, vol. 21, no. 3, 2010, for a typical line of argument.

that technological change that frees information creates an insurmountable challenge to autocrats worldwide[10]. Iran too took measures to extend regime control of the networks and contents. Then, the failed 2009 Green revolution, or "sedition", as Iranian government officials call it, served as a wakeup call for the regime.

The ill-named "Arab Spring" from 2011 served as another proof for Iran that the threat is real. For Russia, Arab revolts were "Colour Revolutions" – an additional proof that the West practices a new and successful form of warfare[11]. Using information to influence and subvert domestic groups, the West succeeds in instigating and steering aggressive interventions into sovereign countries while avoiding costly military confrontation.

The greatest shock for Iran was probably the discovery of the Stuxnet virus in Iran in 2010[12]. This was the first ever destructive cyberattack. Launched by the "devils", the US and Israel, Stuxnet created cascading damage to Iranian self-confidence, in addition to destroying centrifuges in Natanz underground Fuel Enrichment Plant[13]. While some international relations experts downplay Stuxnet's significance, it remains the most effective illustration of cyber threats to date[14]. In September 2011 and again in May 2012, two forms of advanced spyware, Duqu and Flame, respectively, were discovered on computer networks in Iran.

---

[10] Sh. Kalathil and T.C. Boas, *Open Networks, Closed Regimes : The Impact of the Internet on Authoritarian Rule*, Washington D.C., Carnegie Endowment for International Peace, 2003, p. 1; p. 13.

[11] V. Bunce, "The Prospects for a Color Revolution in Russia", *Daedalus*, vol. 146, no. 2, 2017.

[12] K. Zetter, *Countdown to Zero Day: Stuxnet and the Launch of the World's First Digital Weapon*, New York, Crown, 2014.

[13] See an analysis of Israel's cyber power in L. Tabansky and I.B. Israel, *Cybersecurity in Israel*, in *Springerbriefs in Cybersecurity*, Springer International Publishing, ch. 9, 2015; L. Tabansky, "Towards a Theory of Cyber Power: The Israeli Experience with Innovation and Strategy", paper presented at the 8th International Conference on Cyber Conflict (CyCon16), Tallinn, Estonia, 2016.

[14] J.R. Lindsay, "Stuxnet and the Limits of Cyber Warfare", *Security Studies* , vol. 22, no. 3, 2013, pp. 365-404.

Since 2011, Iran's situation has undergone turbulence:

- The rise of Web-enabled communications, online social media, and mobile instant messaging in particular;
- The wave of uprisings in the Middle East;
- The spectacular rise of Daesh and its territorial gains;
- Syria's civil war, and the toll on Hezbollah and Iran during their efforts to defend Assad's regime;
- The growing extent of Iran's control over Iraq, at the expense of American hopes;
- The US-imposed severe financial sanctions on Iran, including blocking access to the SWIFT international money transfer system;
- The 2013 announcement of nuclear negotiations between the P5+1/EU and Iran; the 2015 Joint Comprehensive Plan of Action (JCPOA) and the subsequent lift of economic sanctions;
- Russia's return to Syria and the Middle East;
- Intensified Iran-Saudi Arabia and Iran-Yemen hostilities;
- Donald J. Trump's presidency, renewing American sanctions in response to Iran's ballistic missile testing and aggression in Yemen[15];
- Recent ongoing popular protests throughout Iran's urban centres triggered in part by worsening economic conditions;
- The US withdrawal from the JCPOA (which the President called "the worst deal ever negotiated") and the subsequent American imposition of economic sanctions, consistent with Trump's new strategy towards Iran[16].

---

[15] White House Foreign Policy Fact Sheets, "President Donald J. Trump's First Year of Foreign Policy Accomplishments", Washington, DC, 19 December 2017.

[16] The White House also cited cyber-attacks against the US, Israel, and other American allies in the Middle East as justification for acting against Iran, http://www.whitehouse.gov/briefings-statements/president-donald-j-trumps-new-strategy-iran/

Iran's ambitions, driven by the ideology-driven revolutionary authoritarian regime and Shi'a-Sunna competition, are impressive: to undermine the Western-led international system and to export Iran's ideology throughout the Middle East[17]. As the 2018 US National Defense Strategy states, "In the Middle East, Iran is competing with its neighbours, asserting an arc of influence and instability while vying for regional hegemony, using state-sponsored terrorist activities, a growing network of proxies, and its missile program to achieve its objectives"[18].

Iran's ambitions greatly extend its economy or armed forces. Traditional rivals outgun Iran. Iran spent 3% of its GDP on defence, less than Saudi Arabia (10%), Israel (6%), Iraq (5%), and Jordan (4%)[19]. Iran is in eighth place in the Middle East in terms of defence spending as a percentage of GDP. Iran's spending lags in absolute terms, as well. In 2016, for example, Saudi Arabia spent US$63.7 billion on defence, five times Iran's US$12.7 billion.

The complicated, volatile environment further stressed that gap between goals and means.

This is where strategy plays a crucial role. Iran's Supreme Leader Ali Khamenei and the Islamic Revolutionary Guard Corps (IRGC) incessantly use force and subversion for these goals. Strategic culture has a profound impact on Iran. As Eisenstadt wrote in 2011: "to address both its perceived threats and satisfy its grand strategic ambitions, Iran relies on armed surrogates, large volunteer forces, a 'guerrilla navy', strategic rockets and missiles, and soft power"[20]. Continuing this argument, I focus on how Iran adopts cybered warfare to promote its strategic goals while adhering to its preferences: using

[17] M. Eisenstadt, "The Strategic Culture of the Islamic Republic of Iran: Operational and Policy Implications", Quantico VA, Marine Corps, University Middle East Studies, 2011.

[18] Summary of the National Defense Strategy of the United States of America, 2018.

[19] SIPRI (Stockholm International Peace Research Institute), 2016.

[20] M. Eisenstadt (2011).

proxies and conducting hostilities below the threshold of armed retaliation.

## Means To Achieve the Goals: Cyber Campaigns

Since at least 2009, the Islamic Republic of Iran has regularly responded to sanctions or perceived provocations by conducting offensive cyber campaigns[21]. For years Saudi Arabia, the Netherlands, Germany, Israel, and the United States have discovered and publicly disclosed cyberattacks by Iranian threat actors[22] against their government, military, or scientific institutions. The theft of Web security certificates from the Dutch Certificate Authority (CA)[23] company DigiNotar in July 2011 enabled the attacker to issue rogue certificates with the CA'as full authority. Thus Iranian authorities were able to stage a largescale Man-In-The-Middle (MITM) attack with generated rogue DigiNotar Gmail certificates on an estimated 300,000 Iranian users[24]. Iranian security forces were able to identify presumable secure dissident networks and crack down on them: a massively successful outcome[25].

The August 2012 attack on Saudi Aramco used the Shamoon malware and erased the hard drives of 30,000 corporate computers (although it did not affect industrial SCADA-supervisory control and data acquisition systems)[26]. Two weeks later,

---

[21] G. Levi, S. Chohan, and G. Lesnewich, "Iran's Hacker Hierarchy Exposed: How the Islamic Republic of Iran Uses Contractors and Universities to Conduct Cyber Operations", *CTA*, Recorded Future, 2018.

[22] Threat actor: An individual or group conducting malicious cyber activity. As attribution is complicated, industry and governments first attribute actions to threat actors, which in turn may be linked to governments.

[23] Digital certificates are issued by Certificate Authorities who verify the identity of the entity or person requesting it. Basically, through digital certificates, a user knows whether she can trust the website.

[24] N. Meulen van der, "Diginotar: Dissecting the First Dutch Digital Disaster", *Journal of Strategic Security*, vol. 6, no. 2, 2013.

[25] https://www.theregister.co.uk/2011/09/06/diginotar_audit_damning_fail/

[26] C. Bronk and E. Tikk-Ringas, "The Cyber Attack on Saudi Aramco", *Survival*,

Qatar's RasGas was affected by the virus. These, as well as foiled attacks on Israeli and Saudi power grids, are generally attributed to Iran, which allegedly decided to retaliate for Stuxnet with its own destructive attacks. In September 2012, Iran initiated a series of distributed denial of service (DDoS) attacks, dubbed Operation Ababil, on the websites of the New York Stock Exchange and major US banks[27].

The February 2014 cyberattack on the Las Vegas headquarters of American billionaire Sheldon Adelson's Sands Corporation casino and hotel chain, was Iran's retaliation for a public statement by Adelson the previous October that seemed to call for a nuclear strike on Iran if it did not give up its own nuclear program[28].

The recent Carnegie Endowment for International Peace report strongly suggests that Iran aligns and employs cyber capabilities to pursue its own interests:

> Over the past decade, offensive cyber operations have become a core tool of Iranian statecraft, for the purposes of espionage, signaling, and coercion. [...] Just as Iran uses proxies to project its regional power, Tehran often masks its cyber operations using proxies to maintain plausible deniability[29].

As the JCPOA entered into force, Iran has not diminished its cyber offense to impose costs on its rivals in the Middle East and the West. US Deputy Secretary of Defense Robert Work testified in 2015 that "Iran very likely views its cyber program as one of many tools for carrying out asymmetric but proportional retaliation against political foes"[30]. Moreover, Sulmeyer called

---

vol. 55, no. 2, 2013, pp. 81-96.

[27] R. Levi, "Modern Warfare", *IsraelDefense*, 16 February 2013.

[28] M. Eisenstadt, *Iran's Lengthening Cyber Shadow*, Washington, Institute for Near East Policy, 2016.

[29] *Iran's Cyber Threat: Espionage, Sabotage, and Revenge*, The Carnegie Endowment for International Peace, 4 January 2018.

[30] M. Sulmeyer, "Cyberspace: A Growing Domain for Iranian Disruption", in K.H Hicks and M.G Dalton (eds.), *Deterring Iran after the Nuclear Deal*, Lanham,

for increased vigilance to Iran's cyber power even as JCPOA was in force. Especially given the nuclear accord and UN Security Council Resolution 2231, Iran has less ambiguity in what it cannot do. Iran has continued with the covert procurement of technology for its missile and nuclear programs, missile launch exercises, and arms transfers to proxies and allies in Syria and Yemen[31]. Exploring what activities will not jeopardise sanctions relief and foreign investment, Iran increasingly turned to cyber warfare.

Iran's cyber threat, therefore, is not a new phenomenon. Nor is it likely to fade with the JCPOA.

## A Case Study of Cybered Conflict: The Mabna Institute

Given the rate of technological change and the geopolitical volatility, we must always analyse the latest evidence of Iran's offensive cyber campaign[32]. An indictment made public on March 23 shed light on current Iran's operation (as well as American counterefforts, attribution, and response)[33]. The Mabna Institute was an Iran-based company created in 2013 for the express purpose of gaining access to non-Iranian scientific resources through computer intrusions. Members of the Institute were contracted by the Islamic Revolutionary Guard Corps – one of several defence entities within the Iranian government responsible for gathering intelligence – as well as other Iranian government clients. The US Treasury declared:

---

Maryland, Rowman & Littlefield, 2017.

31 M. Eisenstadt (2016).

32 Campaign is a set of activities carried out by threat actors to achieve a particular purpose, as the KillChain Intrusion model describes. Campaigns include numerous interdependent steps, and is a term much better describing the reality than "attack".

33 https://www.justice.gov/opa/pr/nine-iranians-charged-conducting-massive-cyber-theft-campaign-behalf-islamic-revolutionary

> The Mabna Institute is an Iran-based company that engaged in the theft of personal identifiers and economic resources for private financial gain. The organisation was founded in or about 2013 to assist Iranian universities and scientific and research organisations in obtaining access to non-Iranian scientific resources. The Mabna Institute also contracted with Iranian governmental and private entities to conduct hacking activities on its behalf[34].

According to the FBI, victims of the Mabna Institute included at least approximately:

- 3,768 professors in 144 universities in the US;
- 4,230 professors in 176 foreign universities in 21 countries: Australia, Canada, China, Denmark, Finland, Germany, Ireland, Israel, Italy, Japan, Malaysia, the Netherlands, Norway, Poland, Singapore, South Korea, Spain, Sweden, Switzerland, Turkey, and the United Kingdom;
- Three state government agencies in the US;
- Two federal government agencies in the US;
- 36 private companies in the US;
- 11 foreign private companies;
- Two international non-governmental organisations[35].

The Mabna Institute targeted more than 100,000 accounts of professors in universities around the world. The hackers successfully compromised approximately 8% (8,000) of those accounts. The Mabna Institute coordinated and paid for the hacks. The campaign continued through at least December 2017. Their primary goal was to obtain usernames and passwords for the accounts of professors so they could gain access and proprietary academic information: access to library databases, scientific journals, and electronic books.

---

[34] U.S. Department of the Treasury, "Treasury Sanctions Iranian Cyber Actors for Malicious Cyber-Enabled Activities Targeting Hundreds of Universities", Press Realease, 23 March 2018.

[35] Iranian Mabna Hackers, https://www.fbi.gov/wanted/cyber/iranian-mabna-hackers

Professors' credentials grant access not only to that university networked systems but the global repositories of scientific knowledge. Controlled by a consolidating number of private companies, these databases are prohibitively expensive even for Western users: online access to a single article or chapter is sold for tens of Euros. University libraries are the main clients that purchase annual access for university staff and students. Additionally, US sanctions on Iran may be interpreted as prohibiting access to the databases from Iran. All that scientific information and intellectual property were provided to the Iranian government.

Thus, with a relatively unsophisticated cyber-attack, Iran has been able to target and exploit hundreds of high-value institutions worldwide. Across the 320 universities, Iran has been able to conduct massive espionage and theft of intellectual property (by gaining credentials to access proprietary scholarly publications databases). The exfiltrated data and stolen login credentials acquired through these malicious cyber-enabled activities were used for the benefit of Iran's IRGC. In parallel, the Mabna Institute sold the stolen data through two websites: Megapaper.ir and Gigapaper.ir. Megapaper sold stolen academic resources to customers within Iran, including universities and institutions. Gigapaper sold stolen university professor credentials to customers within Iran to directly access the online library systems of particular foreign universities.

In addition to targeting universities, the hackers gained access to employee e-mail accounts at nearly 50 private companies around the world – the majority of them US firms. Among the US-based victims were academic publishers, media and entertainment companies, technology companies, and investment firms.

The indictment says the university breaches involved "spearfishing" targeted emails to trick users into providing their login credentials. A click on the email link took the victim to an Internet domain that resembled their own university's website and asked them to log in. For the private sector, the indictment says hackers used "password spraying": trying commonly used passwords to access accounts. Both tactics and tools are common, rudimentary, and cost-effective.

Employing rather rudimentary cyber offensive tools, Iran state-sponsored hackers were able to reach globally and steal 31TB of data: roughly three times the amount of data contained in the print collection of the Library of Congress.

## Discussion: Western Defence Failure

The recent report by Carnegie Endowment states:

> Despite its confident claims, Iran is generally perceived as a third-tier cyber power, lacking an advanced indigenous cybersecurity apparatus capable of carrying out sophisticated operations like China, Israel, Russia, and the US – it has effectively exploited the lack of preparedness of targets inside and outside Iran[36].

The nuance in the quote above is a welcome progress, away from a purely technical assessment. While Iran lacks *advanced indigenous* capability, it does achieve results.

My analysis further demonstrates that Iran matures in aligning strategy with tools. In the Mabna Institute case, the goal was to gain (illegal) access to Western science and technology assets and disseminate these it to leapfrog domestic R&D, capacity build-up, and human capital development. For international security, I stress that while Iran may *lack an advanced indigenous cybersecurity apparatus capable of carrying out sophisticated operations* it is able to achieve strategically important goals[37]. The fact that Iran did not need to invest in a costly development process and still was able to successfully use cyber power demonstrates three points:

---

[36] *Iran's Cyber Threat: Espionage, Sabotage, and Revenge*, The Carnegie Endowment for International Peace, 4 January 2018.

[37] North Korea is the best example for arguing against the link from *indigenous* R&D to power: even the retarded state has exploited cyber-warfare for profit and power.

1. technical sophistication does not linearly correlate with mission success[38];
2. Iran continues to use proxies for its strategic offensive purpose: the Mabna Institute seemed a private commercial-criminal enterprise;
3. Western defences tumble down even to an unsophisticated attack.

The questionable effectiveness of Western cyber defences has the broadest range of theoretical and policy implications; I now turn to discuss several aspects of the problem.

From the IT-security perspective, there has been nothing impressive or "cutting edge" in the Mabna Institute cyberattacks. Phishing is the most common and the most cost-effective technique to breach network defences[39]. None of the malware used was unique[40]. The Mabna campaign was executed by seemingly non-state actors, which employed publicly available malware and Tactics, Techniques and Procedures (TTPs). A conclusion that Iran's cyber warfare lacks technical sophistication or elegance is correct. But this of course entirely neglects adversarial intent, strategic alliances between threat actors, and the cyber campaign's effectiveness. However, to deduce from that the threat is low is wrong.

## An Alarming Absence of Western Retaliation

Adversaries are maturing in waging cybered warfare, purposely remaining below the threshold of effective Western response. Iran is another example: it has been able to conduct hostile cyber campaigns in 21 developed countries, and incur damage to universities and the broader national interests.

---

[38] B. Buchanan, "The Legend of Sophistication in Cyber Operations", *Cyber Security Project, Belfer Center*, 2017.

[39] Verizon, *2018 Data Breach Investigations Report*, 2018.

[40] A. Lemay et al., "Survey of Publicly Available Reports on Advanced Persistent Threat Actors", *Computers & Security*, vol. 72, 2018, pp. 26-59.

What has been the responses of the nations that suffered Iran's attack? With publishing evidence and indicting individuals, the US went further than all other countries targeted by the Mabna Institute. The FBI and private actors[41] engaged in an investigation as well as in notifying affected organisations. State-grade capabilities were likely used to create a body of evidence. The Department of Justice prepared and made a criminal indictment. The indictment was unsealed, making many details of US counterefforts public as well as signaling the world that the US can identify and attribute foreign cyber campaigns. The choice of public criminal action and the following economic sanctions also signal the costs the US can impose on the offenders. The Department of the Treasury's Office of Foreign Assets Control (OFAC) designated the Mabna Institute and the nine defendants for sanctions for the malicious cyber-enabled activity outlined in the Indictment.

> Iran is engaged in an ongoing campaign of malicious cyber activity against the US and our allies. The IRGC outsourced cyber intrusions to The Mabna Institute, a hacker network that infiltrated hundreds of universities to steal sensitive data", said Treasury Under Secretary Sigal Mandelker[42].

Despite the indictment, the Mabna Institute continues to operate without interruption. Some may choose to criticise the US for inadequate response. However, this would miss the point.

20 of the 21 countries that have suffered the attack's damage have not taken any substantial action against the foreign state that is responsible for the attack. Among these 20, Italy and

---

[41] C. Hassold, *Silent Librarian: More to the Story of the Iranian Mabna Institute Indictmen*, The PhishLabs Blog, 26 marzo 2018; Id., *Silent Librarian University Attacks Continue Unabated in Days Following Indictment*, The PhishLabs Blog, 5 April 2018.

[42] https://home.treasury.gov/news/press-releases/sm0332, Treasury Sanctions Iranian Cyber Actors for Malicious Cyber-Enabled Activities Targeting Hundreds of Universities, Press Release.

Israel have both failed not only in cyber defence[43] but also in punishment, signaling, and deterrence.

## The Use of Proxies Works for Iran

Since 1979, Iran's actions targeting perceived adversaries' foreign policy has been conducted by proxies. What the West terms "convergence of illicit networks" are the norm, not the exception, for Iran. Iran's former cultural attaché in Argentina, Mohsen Rabbani, is the leading suspect behind the 1994 bombing of a Jewish community centre in Buenos Aires that killed 85 people and injured hundreds. Iran's proxy militias play a prominent role in Tehran's political warfare strategy. Iran's expeditionary force, the Islamic Revolutionary Guards Corps Quds Force (IRGC-QF), is responsible for training pro-Iranian militants across the Middle East and beyond[44]. Lebanese Hezbollah is the most successful example of Iran's proxy strategy. Hezbollah is one of Iran's instruments of power and forward defences, employed to contain Israel. Simultaneously, Hezbollah is a sectarian grassroots Shi'a movement, a Lebanese political party, and a global drug dealing and money laundering conglomerate. Hezbollah has enjoyed heavy support from Iran – including the supply of tens of thousands of rockets and missiles, among them the most advanced parts in Iran's arsenal. With Syria's civil war, Iran has been able to deploy the Shiite Hezbollah to a new task: provide large military support to the Bashar al-Assad Alawi regime. Hezbollah has deployed some 6,000 fighters to the areas around Damascus, Homs, Aleppo, and Hama. Hezbollah has performed Iran's mission despite the heavy losses: some 20% killed. In Syria, Iran has been able to also deploy other proxies. By the fall of 2012, thousands of Iraqi Shi'a militants were

[43] I am not aware of any increase in government support to defend universities from state-grade cyber attackers in either Italy or Israel.

[44] L. Robinson et al., *Modern Political Warfare: Current Practices and Possible Responses*, RAND Corporation, 2018.

travelling to Iran and then being flown to Damascus to fight for Assad. Then in early 2014, Iran showed its ability to deploy Afghan Shi'a fighters to replace the Iraqi Shi'a militants who had returned to Iraq to fight Daesh. The post-victory presence of Iranian elite forces in Syria is among the current Israel's red lines. In fact, Israel has been able to navigate the complex web of Russian and Western interests in Syria to continue to operate from the air against this Iranian threat.[45] While proxies are smaller, less professional, and less reliable than regular armies, they played a crucial role in winning the war.

Aside from the Houthi rebels in Yemen, Shi'a militias in Iraq and Syria and Hezbollah everywhere else, in cyber warfare the role of proxies is at least as central for Iran. In cyber, similarly, proxies may be less professional and less reliable. Yet, the Mabna Institute has delivered value that serves the strategic goals, all the while operating below the Western threshold of armed retaliation.

## Is Conceptual Disarray to Blame?

The Mabna Institute exploiting targets in 22 countries demonstrated again the Western failure in providing comprehensive national cybersecurity even against less-sophisticated adversaries. Indeed, national cybersecurity in the civilian sector has many substantial challenges[46]. Universities, the main research institutions that produce innovation, naturally are a prime target for numerous threat actors conducting scientific, military, and industrial espionage. Universities are also notoriously difficult to govern, suffer continuing budget deficits, and tend to

---

[45] https://www.longwarjournal.org/archives/2018/04/israel-kills-iranian-guard-corps-members-in-syria.php; https://www.theatlantic.com/international/archive/2018/04/syria-israel/557855/

[46] For national analyses, see G. Austin, *Cybersecurity in China: The Next Wave*, Springer, 2018; M. Schallbruch and I. Skierka, *Cybersecurity in Germany*, Springer, 2018; L.Tabansky and I. Ben-Israel (2015); M. Dunn Cavelty, *Cybersecurity in Switzerland*, Springer, 2014.

outsource administrative positions such as IT. Unlike financial institutions, universities are not subject to a strict IT security compliance regime, nor are they considered critical infrastructure in the advanced countries. Moreover, the staunch autonomous stance which protects academic freedom has also contributed to universities' reluctance to adopt more effective IT-security solutions. Thus, most universities are a soft target: their networks and users have not been up to speed in IT security. The defence problems of national cybersecurity are not the focus of this paper. In international conflict, and especially within Iran's context, it is important to examine the effect of the conceptual disarray that hinders Western defence.

The West enjoys an enviable security environment. All recent threats, including suicide terrorism, Daesh, lawfare[47], political warfare[48], "fake news," energy supply, and cyberattacks are dominating Western national security agendas. But this happens because the traditional threats have long disappeared. None of these threats are existential; all pale in comparison to conventional, let alone nuclear, interstate wars. We thus assign these to a category below "proper" warfare. Western and especially NATO pundits increasingly call these threats "hybrid" warfare[49]. The way Western and NATO observers consider cyber power, they tend to put cyber threats at a level below the threshold of "proper war". Hybrid implies lesser responsibility of any of traditional defenders.

However, this conceptual disarray is counterproductive. A change in security environment can trigger defence adaptation. In practice, it is instead often abused to avoid serious changes in national defence. Debates are raging on the proper nature

---

[47] O.F. Kittrie, *Lawfare : Law as a Weapon of War*, Oxford - New York NY, Oxford University Press, 2016.

[48] L. Robinson et al. (2018).

[49] W. Murray and P.R Mansoor, *Hybrid Warfare: Fighting Complex Opponents from the Ancient World to the Present*, Cambridge, Cambridge University Press, 2012; J.N. Mattis and F. Hoffman, "Future Warfare: The Rise of Hybrid Wars", *Proceedings-United States Naval Institute*, vol. 131, no. 11, 2005, pp. 42-49.

of these threats, often suggesting that defence transformation should wait until a commonly accepted definition emerges. Western defence terms are aligned with organisation. Each existing security organisation – armed forces, law enforcement, counter-espionage, counter-subversion – has long-standing missions. Each organisation lawfully and reasonably focuses on the existing tasks. When demands to deal with additional mission arise, each organisation offers to use its existing methods. None of these are fully compatible with providing national cybersecurity, as our societies would not accept a blow to fundamental freedoms. The privacy-security dilemmas in cybersecurity are the clearest illustration. The common feature is that the Western states have repeatedly failed to effectively mitigate non-military threats, most recently cybered threats. As defence priorities have not been realigned with reality, it is not a lack of resources but conceptual disarray further that obstructs our own capacity to respond effectively to foreign state-sponsored cyberattacks.

## Crime-State Nexus *vs* Western Binary State/Non-State Categorisation

Western defenders continue to struggle with attribution of cyberattacks. Part of the problem lays in the fixation to improve technical forensics and identify the individuals behind the keyboard. A second part is the legalese jumble, which often wrongly adopts criminal law standards to establish a connection between these individuals and the state. Again, Iran's attackers were not part of a state apparatus, but rather an alliance between criminals, hackers, and state-affiliated individuals. This attests to lower capabilities, and more importantly, serves to provide "plausible deniability" which attracts the sizeable attention of cyber deterrence theorists.

Is plausible deniability really justified? Evidence on Iran's actions reiterates the need to move beyond a binary state/non-state approach to attribution and responsibility. It is essential to develop approaches that better reflect reality. One such approach is readily available in Healey's 2012 "Beyond attribution: seeking national responsibility for cyberattacks"[50]. Healey proposes the use of a Spectrum of State Responsibility: a tool to help analysts with imperfect knowledge assign responsibility for a particular attack, or campaign of attacks, with more precision and transparency. Healey's spectrum covers ten categories, based on whether a nation ignores, abets, or conducts an attack.

1. The national government will help stop the third-party attack;
2. The national government is cooperative but unable to stop the third-party attack;
3. The national government knows about the third-party attack but is unwilling to take any official action;
4. Third parties control and conduct the attack, but the national government encourages them as a matter of policy;
5. Third parties control and conduct the attack, but the state provides some support;
6. The national government coordinates third-party attackers such as by "suggesting" operational details;
7. The national government directs third-party proxies to conduct the attack on its behalf;
8. State-rogue-conducted. Out-of-control elements of cyber forces of the national government conduct the attack;
9. State-executed. The national government conducts the attack using cyber forces under its direct control;
10. State-integrated. The national government attacks using integrated third-party proxies and government cyber forces.

[50] J. Healey, "Beyond Attribution: Seeking National Responsibility for Cyber Attacks", in *Cyber Statecraft Initiative*, Washington D.C., Atlantic Council, 2012.

Let us exercise in applying this framework. From the indictment, it looks like the Mabna Institute acted at stage 4 (at the very least): it was the third party that controls and conducts the attack, but the national government encouraged it as a matter of policy. From what is known, though, it is more likely that the Mabna Institute acted at stage 6: Iran's intelligence may weakly have supported the campaign with valuable information. With further evidence, we may even reach the conclusion that the Mabna Institute operated at stage 10 (state-integrated). This short exercise in moving forward from the binary distinction shows its value. Iran's national responsibility becomes much clearer and much more granular. This framework is readily available to dismiss the artificial obstacles to a possible Western response.

## Conclusion: The Consequences of a Repetitive Losing Game

Iran's Mabna Institute is a current example of cyber power: using cyber technology to create advantages and influence events in other operational environments and across the instruments of power.

Iran's deterrence has had three pillars:

1. The disruption in maritime traffic passing through the Strait of Hormuz;
2. Unilateral and proxy terrorist attacks on several continents;
3. The launch of long-range missiles and rocket strikes against targets throughout the region[51].

In the aftermath of Assad's victory in the Syrian civil war, Iran, with its heavy use of proxies, has demonstrated a power-projection capability within the Middle East.

---

[51] M. Eisenstadt, "The Strategic Culture of the Islamic Republic of Iran: Operational and Policy Implications", Quantico VA, Marine Corps, University.

**1. Forward deployment of proxies is now the forth deterrent pillar**

I have argued that the growing scope and effectiveness of Iran's offensive cyber operations is still met with near-zero retaliation. The lack of effective Western response definitely plays a crucial role in cybered conflicts. As long as Western defences remain inadequate, the attractiveness of cyber offense to Iran will continue to grow.

**2. I expect that cyber offense will soon become an additional pillar of Iran's power**

Iran's cyber threat, therefore, is not a new phenomenon. Nor is it likely to fade. On the other hand, Western nations have failed to defend and to deter the aggressor. Each time Western political, economic, and societal values might appear paralysed, we lose: the Western model loses public appeal at home as well as squanders credibility on the global stage. Every nation that values its security and sovereignty has no choice but to start experimenting with new ways and work towards national cybersecurity. This straightforward approach to advance national cybersecurity is long overdue. Both Italy and Israel possess sizeable relevant independent capabilities to project power against "hybrid" adversaries. In some areas, fusing the relative advantages of Italy and Israel will yield dramatic benefits for both – and for the Western alliance.

# 6. The Balance of Power in Cyberspace

Umberto Gori

## The Balance of Power and Interpretation Models

According to Henry Kissinger[1], "our age is insistently, at times almost desperately, in pursuit of a concept of a world order", and the new information and communication technologies "projects events globally, but in a manner that inhibits reflections, demanding of leaders that they register instantaneous reactions in a form expressible in slogans". And he wonders: "Are we facing a period in which forces beyond the restraints of any order determine the future?".

When addressing the international order, despite the many interpretations by different cultures, we actually refer to the balance of power as conceived in the XVII century at Westphalia, following a century of disorder and bloody conflicts. "No truly global world order has ever existed", argues the former Secretary of State.

The question is: is a balance of power (BoP) possible in the cyber age? Or, in other words, which are the conditions for a balance of power and which are the differences between a traditional balance of power and a cyber balance of power?

It should be mentioned that such a balancing system has been avowed until World War II in a multilateral context and

---

[1] H. Kissinger, *World Order*, Penguin Books, 2014, p. 2.

– since then and until 1991 – in the Cold War bilateral framework. Afterward, and for a long period, the expression "post-bipolarism" emerged, followed by "unipolarism", and more recently by a revival of "multipolarism" or, better, of "a-polarism", to the G-Zero world, where nobody holds the leadership. (J. Bremmer). The world, therefore, has not an order yet.

The Westphalia's balance of power[2] had two specific goals: to retain or restore a constant balance in the international system; and to preserve the original crucial actors (five was the magic number, according to Kaplan)[3] of the system, or to replace them, possibly upgrading a "small" State to the "crucial actor" level, in order to ensure the system balance and the systemic one (as inferred by Gilpin). The presence of an actor who can "tip the scale" according to the needs enabled the system to work smoothly despite having been criticised for fostering pre-emptive, Clausewitz-like conflicts[4]. The opposite argument

---

[2] On the principles and techniques of the BoP amplius in U. Gori, Corso di Relazioni Internazionali, Università degli Studi di Firenze, Facoltà di Scienze Politiche "Cesare Alfieri", Anno Accademico 1970-71; and Id., *Lezioni di Relazioni Internazionali*, second edition, CEDAM, 2004. An endless number of books deal with the subject. Among the most important see H. Morgenthau, *Politics among Nations*, New York, Knopf, 1973; I.L. Claude Jr., *Power and International relations*, New York, Random House, 1962; K.N. Waltz, *Theory of International Politics*, New York, McGraw-Hills, 1979; J.J. Mearsheimer, *The Tragedy of Great Power Politics*, New York, W.W. Norton & Co., 2001; R. Gilpin, *War and Change in World Politics*, Cambridge, Cambridge University Press, 1981; A.F.K. Organski, *World Politics*, New York, Knopf, 1958. In literature there are up to nine different meanings of BoP (Waltz, p. 117). For Claude it is "an ambiguous concept" (p. 19). As to Mearsheimer, "the balance of power is largely synonymous with the balance of military power" (p. 56). For an overview of the evolution of the balance of power theory, see R.L. Schweller, *The Balance of Power in World Politics*, Oxford, Oxford University Press, 2016. According to Susan Strange, the BoP shifted away from states to world markets. *The retreat of the State – The Diffusion of Power in the World Economy*, Cambridge, Cambridge University Press, 1996.

[3] M.A. Kaplan, *System and Process in International Politics*, J. Wiley & Sons, New York, 1957; "Balance of Power, Bipolarity and Other Models of International Systems", *The American Political Science Review*, vol. 51, no. 3, 1957, pp. 684-95.

[4] "Most of the wars that have been fought since the beginning of the modern state system have their origin in the balance of power", H. Morgenthau (1973), p. 210.

is that we cannot acknowledge how many wars it has averted.

Initially a uniquely European concept – even though Morgenthau dates it back to more than two thousand years ago – the balance of power eventually developed at a global level. Traditionally, this change dates back to the Monroe Doctrine in 1823, or to the Canning Government' statement of 1826 in front of the British Parliament after being charged with having allowed France to alter the European balance. Canning argued that the balance was in the world's outskirts. However, the decolonisation process erased the concept of outskirts, as well as the significant reduction of key actors and the globalisation process erased the "tip the scale" element.

One of the most relevant criteria underlying the European balance of power and explaining its duration is a certain degree of cultural homogeneity and, therefore, a common rationale: features that largely persist even after 1945 with just two key actors.

Legitimacy and national sovereignty, non-interference in States' domestic affairs, and diplomatic immunity for the enhancement of conflict reduction communication are the most important Westphalian principles.

We should also keep in mind that among the preconditions of the traditional balance of power we find the belief – actually, the awareness – that States are the true actors of an international system characterised by anarchy, and that power is defined only as military strength. However, as Kissinger argued, the balance of power "is not a celebration of power but rather an attempt to limit its use". If needed, the power of each State is counterbalanced by the creation of coalitions or other balancing means, in order to avoid the rise of hegemonic powers. Historically, this was Great Britain's primary role as the country that can tip the scale. In case of failure, the final solution was the outburst of a war. In other words, the balance of power was grounded in compromise. As argued by Kissinger, "the greatest need of the contemporary international system is an agreed concept of order. In its absence, the awesome available power is unrestrained by any consensus as to legitimacy [...] without it stability will prove elusive"[5].

In this context, the input of the traditional realist paradigm of international relations is obvious. But in a new global context characterised by pervasive technologies and information, communications and technology (ICT) tools, where the power assessment is not grounded in traditional military tools, and where the States' monopoly is a concept of the past, it seems necessary to turn to different explanatory models. States do not surrender the military power, but they increasingly resort to soft power – the relational power – even though some people argue that the soft power age is over and we are back to the "hard" one[6].

In the most recent years, the international order has undertaken a radical transformation. The new post-international politics is characterised by complex interdependence and (deterministic) chaos. Uncertainty is the result. Another consequence is the extension of the concept of security. So-called unexpected events are more and more recurring, and small incidents cause abnormal consequences. The only way to control the change and win the turbulence is a sophisticated resilience capacity.

In my opinion, the model that best explains modern complexity is the turbulence one[7]. On this ground, the contemporary international system should be analysed through the chaos and complexity mathematics, and anyway with the computational social science tools.

We will see below which is the most appropriate paradigm to address, to some extent, the power of balance in the cyber age.

---

[5] H. Kissinger, *Central Issues of American Foreign Policy, Foreign Relations of the United States*, 1959-74, vol. 1, Foundations of Foreign policy, 1969-72.

[6] E. Li, "Il soft power Americano è morto: riuscirà la Cina a sostituirlo?", *Limes*, 6/2018, pp. 263-70.

[7] J.N. Rosenau, "Turbulence in World Politics: A Theory of Change and Continuity", Princeton University Press, 1990. A comment of this theory is in U. Gori (2004), pp. 74-81.

## Cyberspace

This is the framework in which cyberspace developed, the only space entirely created and adaptable by humankind. Unlike during the Cold War era, when wars were conveyed to proxy States, it offers the option of a direct conflict [8].

Big changes in international politics are due to three factors: conflicts, economic change, and technology development, with a subsequent transfer of resources. Likewise, and increasingly, IC technology is changing – to what extent it is difficult to say – the relationship dynamics among States: it modifies the whole architecture of the international system, changes the traditional process (for example, the digital diplomacy entails a radical transformation of the communication process), overturns finance, trade, and sensitive data gathered by intelligence services, is a source of new problems for foreign politics (WikiLeaks, for example), changes and speeds up the perception of significant events related to security. In addition, ICT is accessible to subnational entities and individuals and enables the latter to take on a leading role in change, thus stealing the monopoly of control and use of force from the States[9].

Consistently with the cyber age, the conflict too has turned from physical into virtual. Today, everything is becoming intangible. Here are the new or "post-modern" wars, as defined by Mary Kaldor [10], asymmetric and low-intensity conflicts (see the

---

[8] Yet, A.L. Shapiro (*The Disappearance of Cyberspace and the Rise of Code*, Harvard Law School, 1998) argues that cyberspace is not a 'place' separate from the physical realm, but rather a place of "control". In fact, "cyber" derives from cybernetics, the science of communication and control theory (from the ancient Greek word "kubernetes" which means "steersman"). This view of cyberspace as a non-autonomous place may have legal implications.

[9] "If non-States or transnational actors are powerful enough to challenge State actors, power configuration in the world may no longer be considered in terms of polarity, but, instead, in terms of the number of layers of policy networks", M. Sun, *Dissertation*, University of Pennsylvania, 2013-14, Website E-International Relations Students.

[10] M.H. Kaldor, *New and Old Wars: Organized Violence in a Global Era*, Stanford CA,

decreasing use of physical force) that blur the clear distinction between "domestic" and "international", grounded in identity claims rather than on territory (here, too, we are moving from tangible to abstract). Conflicts in cyberspace – which, after land, sea, air, and space, is the fifth dimension of international relations – are part of this category[11].

Chaos management requires an identification of the causes of turbulence through early warning systems, a reaction through key scenarios and a choice of strategy based on scenarios priority and risk endurance. We need to pay attention to small warnings and persistently monitor the situation.

Actually, complex systems are not at all inexplicable. Even though accurate forecasts are not possible, mathematics-based models and computer simulations showed the existence of a subjacent order and that we just need some "theoretical blocks" in order to get some forecasts that significantly reduce uncertainty. Nowadays forecasting is supported by big data analysis[12].

Cyberspace owns amazing characteristics: it is cheap, it protects anonymity, it enables attacks from a long distance, from everywhere, and at an incredible speed[13], and its scope is persistently enhanced by the coming up of new Internet users. Furthermore, cyberspace is replacing conventional time with real time; it goes beyond geographic boundaries and physical location; it breaks into borders and legal systems; it is fluid, it changes, and is rapidly resetting; it tears down any obstacle to political activities and participation; it hides the actors' identity and connections identification (the so-called attribution

---

Stanford University Press, 3rd ed., 2012

[11] Cfr. U. Gori, "Cyberspazio e relazioni internazionali: implicazioni geopolitiche e geostrategiche", in U.Gori and S. Lisi (eds.), *Armi cibernetiche e processi decisionali*, Milan, FrancoAngeli, 2013, p. 17; U. Gori (ed.), *Modelling Cyber Security: Approaches, Methodology, Strategies*, NATO, IOS Press, 2009.

[12] See V. Mayer-Schoenberger and K. Cukier, *Big Data*, Boston, Houghton Mifflin Hartcourt, 2013.

[13] The properties of cyberspace severely limit the OODA process, with the result of taking decisions under stress, and therefore sub-optimal or even counter-productive.

problem); it bypasses responsibility mechanisms[14].

Hence, as it always happened in history, technology is the key explanatory variable to understand international relations and power change. In the globalised world and in the cyber age, those who are most technologically advanced will prevail, as it happened in the XIX century when England dominated the Seas and in the XX century when the US owned the air superiority and the best force projection.

State operations are increasingly "virtual"[15], and investments in knowledge and innovation are a primary source of power. This entails a "revolution in diplomatic affairs", which will be ever more grounded in soft power and – on the whole – on tools that are less and less "physical".

Many more ongoing processes will produce important changes that will alter the balance of power. The pivot of power is moving from the Atlantic to Asia and the Pacific, whereas the international system from post-bipolar has already turned into multi-polar or – according to some scholars – a-polar, with the ensuing decline of the US hegemony.

Globalisation processes, prompted by increasing technology development, will inevitably enhance interdependence, with not always positive outcomes. Intra-State and proxy conflicts are the most likely to occur, according to some intelligence agencies.

## Cultures and Strategies

We mentioned the distinctive characteristics of cyberspace and the many subjects that act and clash in such a field. Before addressing the issue of a possible – theoretical and realistic – cyber

[14] See N. Choucri, *Cyberpolitics in International Relations*, Cambridge, Massachusetts, The MIT Press, 2012, p. 4 ss.

[15] For instance, the low cost of offensive cyber weapons allows weak States to modify the balance to their advantage. Quite the opposite, the development of Stuxnet costed as much as US$300 million, according to experts.

balance of power, we should inevitably question the feasibility of the traditional principles of strategy in the new context, in the light of the above-mentioned radical changes.

Before that, we need to better understand the opponent's culture. However, this is a thorny issue because other people's culture is explained according to interpretation models that are different from those of the culture under examination; therefore, a reading would be quite different from a true interpretation of that culture.

A strategy is the outcome of a specific culture and is responsive to the characteristics of the area of competition.

There are two opposing cultural traditions: the Western tradition, which refers to Clausewitz, and the Eastern one (especially Chinese), coming from the ancient teachings of Sun Tzu.

Which one of these two traditions is more viable as to the asymmetric and "fluid" conflicts of the cyber world?

Clausewitz's ideas were – and still are – consistent with the reality of an international framework characterised by sovereign States, divided by political borders as a result of previous conflicts fought with kinetic weapons. According to the Prussian General, war is an act of force, the ultimate force, to subjugate the enemy. Even if considered the "extension of politics through other means", war is in itself a zero-sum game (such as, for example, a chess game).

Broadly speaking, a strategy is a mindset method that implies a specific procedure: such a method allows to assess the situation and to classify and hierarchically rank the events by spotting, whenever possible, frequency and sequence (political diagnostics), to establish political goals (political outline), to express an opinion on options (strategic diagnostics) and, lastly, to set strategic goals and the means to reach them (strategic policy). In short, a strategy is the use of one's own power factors, material and immaterial, and the exploitation of the enemy's vulnerabilities, and all this for political goals[16].

---

[16] I am indebted to so many authors and experts of strategy, making it difficult to mention and thank all of them. Nevertheless, I want to quote some of them: F. Sanfelice di Monteforte, *Strategy and Peace*, Rome, Aracne, 2007; *La Strategia*,

So, Western culture – our culture – is accustomed to addressing challenges straightforwardly, targeting the main goal for achievement, according to Clausewitz's *Schwerpunkt* teaching[17]. Technology, more specifically ICT, has overturned it all. Cyberspace has no borders, and the overwhelming majority of the cyber structure is privately owned. And force cannot be employed when the enemy is invisible and unknown. Furthermore, as Giulio Douhet stated, "the form of any conflict depends on the technical tools available".

On the contrary, Sun Tzu's teaching, in line with the ancient Chinese culture, emphasised the use of intelligence and deceit. According to the ancient strategist, the best general is the one who wins the war without fighting and losses of human lives for his army and for the enemy's one. The goal is the mind of the enemy, and the strategic picture can change by exploiting the potential of each situation and circumstance and by resorting to different tricks. The most ancient board game, the *Go*, is a case in point. *Go* consists of a chessboard over which black and white stones – of the same importance – interact: the stones represent yin and yang, the complementary and interdependent elements that break into the other's territory through a smooth movement similar to the one of water. In this game, like in war, 100% victory is almost impossible, and actions that

Rome, Rubettino, 2010; *Le strategie declaratorie della NATO e dell'UE – Analisi dei concetti strategici*, Rome, Aracne, 2014; B.H. Liddell Hart, *Strategy*, second revised edition, A Meridian Book, 1991; E. de La Maisonneuve, *Stratégie, Crise et Caos*, Economica, 2005; H. Coutau-Bégarie, *Traité de Stratégie*, 6e édition, Economica, 2008; G. Chaliand, *Anthologie Mondiale de la Stratégie: des Origines au Nucléaire*, Paris, R. Laffont, 1990; A. Beaufre, *Introduction a la Stratégie*, Paris, A. Colin, 1963; C. Jean, *Guerra, Strategia e Sicurezza*, Rome-Bari, Laterza, 1997; *Studi Strategici*, Milan, FrancoAngeli, 1990; C. Jean (ed.), *Il pensiero strategico*, Milan, FrancoAngeli, 1985; E. Luttwak, *Strategia - La Logica della Guerra e della Pace*, seconda edizione, Milan, Rizzoli, 2001; C.S. Gray, *Strategic Studies – A Critical Assessment*, Aldwych Press, 1982. The Chinese strategy is described in F. Mini, *L'Altra Strategia – I classici del pensiero militare cinese dalla Guerra al marketing*, Milan, FrancoAngeli, 1998.

[17] The Chinese strategy is based on the idea of the absence of the Clausewitzian "Friktion".

are too aggressive can lead to disaster. The goal is to acquire an ever-increasing share of territory, in order to achieve, in time, a firm strategic position. This is what China is doing with the artificial islands in the Pacific. It resorts to a long-term strategy instead of the use of force. In short, according to the Chinese military thinking, a strategy should exploit the natural trend of things and get ready to change the playground.

Unlike the Western military thinking that sees the strategic environment according to a Newtonian vision with specific physical laws and exploits the principles of mass and manoeuvers, the Eastern thinking takes into consideration the relations among things, that is, the network, which is after all the very structure of the cyber world[18].

Eastern culture addresses challenges in an indirect way, through a strategy based on outcomes, according to the ancient teaching of Sun Tzu, by exploiting the context, the environment, and the overall picture. In other words, for Western people, the goal is the target, while for Eastern people the goal is the entire system. If we consider the danger not in itself but as part of a system, the structure's resilience is enhanced. In other words, as already mentioned, instead of forcing a strategic plan on reality (Western method), the Chinese strategist does not plan but assess and calculate – starting from an accurate analysis of the available forces – all the positive elements for each side that will lead to victory. Thus, letting developments take their course. The action outcome, therefore, is not likely but unavoidable. Only in the Western approach strategy is a theory of action. In the Eastern one, the action shakes the natural evolution of things.

Hence, the conclusion seems to support the Eastern approach as the most suited to address non-kinetic conflicts, whereas the Western one better deals with conflicts with traditional weapons.

---

[18] The Chinese strategy is based on the idea of the absence of the Clausewitzian 'Friktion'.

Let's now address the principles of the Western cultural strategy that I will briefly mention in order to eventually assess their validity in the cyber context.

As we all know, these are: initiative or activity, a concentration of forces on a specific spot; means of economy, exclusivity of goal, mass, and security.

To this, we must add two main elements: time and space.

In a cyber context, the first principle is feasible only in case of a hot cyberwar. In normal conditions, its implementation is not advisable, or even forbidden, by convenience, by procedures, or by law. The second principle makes little sense in a virtual context, and the other principles as well are affected by the immaterial context.

A deep insight should, instead, be put on the time and space aspects, which are basically nonexistent in the cyber domain.

A US Department of Defense document of January 2013 (Resilient Military Systems and the Advanced Cyber Threats) states that cyber threats are an extremely serious issue, with possible consequences similar to those of nuclear threats.

If the comparison between the consequences of cyber and nuclear weapons is to be deemed appropriate, nonetheless two differences arise: the first is the invisibility of the current threat, which entails little understanding of the danger; the second is the rapidity without notice of a possible cyberattack, unlike the nuclear attack for which there are warnings and at least a few-minute time. In conclusion, the current situation is worse. What can protect us is the psychological strain of the opposing parties, as it happened in the nuclear age, to overcome the point of no return. But remember: the Cold War system was characterised by rational actors, the cyber system is crowded with irrational actors or, better, of different rationality. More specifically, I am referring to terrorists. Furthermore, the nuclear system was symmetric, the cyber one is extremely asymmetric, and the weak party often prevails on the strong one. Let's not forget, also, that while the operational doctrine of nuclear weapons implies its non-use, one of the cyber weapons is its problematic use before it is too late, euphemistically speaking the so-called active defence[19].

Other differences arise when considering the specifics of the cyber maneuvers. In short, these are: instant speed, invisibility, unlimited operational range, access to and control of others' systems, dynamic development, quick expansion to unlimited points (for instance, DDoS-distributed denial of service), simultaneous attacks against multiple targets.

It should be stressed the possibility to carry out cyber maneuvers against friendly and allied countries, unlike the kinetic maneuvers that cannot be employed against them. In a conventional context, unpunished actions in cyberspace would be often considered as acts of war.

## Deterrence, Resilience, and Perception

It is widely known that traditional deterrence does not work, for several reasons (attribution issue, etc.), for cyberspace. That is why it is better to talk about countermeasures that – in addition to some sort of cyber retaliation against well-defined and organised entities[20] – include cyber maneuvers, intelligence and kinetic operations, and resilience. The only type of deterrence in cyberspace is by denial. After all, the deterrence aspect is a variable dependent on perception. Its effects are in place even in case of mere political declarations, that is, through announcements that stress the will to respond to destructive attacks with all the necessary means, as highlighted – among others – by the United States and Russia. Let's keep in mind, though, that no announced retaliation will prevent destructive attacks by the would-be martyrs.

---

[19] See also U. Gori, *Manovre nel cyberspazio: prospettive*, in U. Gori and S. Lisi (eds.), *Manovre cibernetiche: impatto sulla sicurezza nazionale*, Milan, FrancoAngeli, 2016.

[20] C. Cioffi-Revilla, "Modelling Deterrence in Cyberia", in U. Gori (ed.), *Modelling Cyber Security: Approaches, Methodology, Strategies*, NATO, IOS Press, 2009, pp. 125-31.

The above-mentioned attribution issue is more easily addressed when a State is involved in the attack. The revealing elements are the situation and the strategic context, the level of consequences, the planning complexity required, and the realpolitik involved[21].

In order to assess the feasibility of a cyber balance of power, it is necessary to take into consideration the issue of perception. On the one hand, it "generates" the reality, that is, an active process of the mind. In other words, we react according to what we perceive in relation to our cultural models and aversions. On the other hand, it allows the assessment of the immaterial extent of the power of a State.

Ray Cline, former CIA Director, formulated the concept of "perceived power": Pp=(D+M+E)x(S+W), where D is the country dimension (territory and population), M is the military structure, and E is the economic and industrial one. These are the material and computable power factors, but they must be weighed up in relation to S, that is, strategy, and W, willingness and, therefore, respectively the existence of a strategy or the lack of it on the side of the assessed country, leadership quality, and national character.

Because they are intangible, the last two elements can only be perceived from the outside, and they are counted on a continuum from 0 to 2.

In the cyber age, these are the elements that weigh more, so that they double or decrease to zero the quantity and quality of the material power factors[22].

Clearly, in the cyber age, the preconditions of the balance of power that take into consideration the States as the only relevant actors in the international system and explain power as military power do not conform with reality anymore. There

---

[21] U. Gori, "L'inarrestabile sviluppo delle armi cibernetiche", in U. Gori and S. Lisi (eds.) (2015), pp.11-17.

[22] See E.L. Armistead, *Suggestions to measure cyberpower and proposed metrics for cyber warfare operations (cyberdeterrence/cyberpower)*, 2016 International Conference on Cyber Conflict (CyCon US), 21-23 October 2016, IEEE, 2017.

are many key actors in the info-sphere and power has different features.

As to the power balance, therefore, Morgenthau and Waltz's realist and neo-realist paradigm (or structural realism) must leave the place to Keohane and Nye's neo-liberal school[23], which stresses the transnational relations where the military power (hard power) is less important. As stated by Parag Khanna, "the XIX century world was led by few key powers that governed their respective colonies, and the XX century one by two opposing blocs. However, in the 21st century, the idea that the world order might be manipulated from above is simply unrealistic". So, we are moving "towards a shattered, fragmented, ungovernable, multipolar, or non-polar world, like in a new Middle Age"[24]. In our times "the de jure world of political borders is about to be replaced by a de facto world of functional connections"[25].

An assumption of the balance of power theory is the rational behaviour of the States which turns into a maximisation of its own security or of power in an anarchical context. A second assumption is the (military) power distributed more or less evenly among the system actors.

Today, an ethical and juridical evolution and the use of soft power entail that the States do not feel the threat of physical extinction. Other key elements, though, are involved – such as, for example, the economic one – and their importance in cyberspace must be assessed.

Joseph Samuel Nye[26] defined cyber power as the only hybrid regime of material (infrastructure, resources, etc.) and virtual assets that can be activated at many levels. The "hard" way for its activation is, however, the one that implies attacks that block

---

[23] R.O. Keohane and J.S. Nye, *Power and Interdependence*, London, Pearson, 2011.

[24] P. Khanna, *Come si comanda il mondo*, Roma, Fazi Editore, 2011, pp. 9 and 18.

[25] P. Khanna, *Connectography – Le mappe del futuro ordine mondiale*, Roma, Fazi Editore, 2016, p. 48.

[26] J. S. Nye Jr, *Cyber Power*, Belfer Center for Science and International Affairs, Harvard Kennedy School, , 2010, pp. 7-8.

data availability or that damage their integrity through DDoS or malware. But even if the nature of the outcomes is similar to kinetic outcomes, it is often questioned.

And here we include the definition issue of cyber weapons. Some of them, for example as Stuxnet against SCADA (supervisory control and data acquisition) systems, are definitely cyber weapons, but many others pave the way to unsolved debates. However, the assessment of the elements of cyber power of the States is complicated due to the secrecy surrounding the construction and the ownership of these weapons. To this purpose, intelligence activity, though difficult, can be pivotal.

Indeed, I am not claiming to have a final solution to the issue, but in my opinion, a cyber tool is a weapon if it is virtually lethal, that is, destructive for things and people. Of course, we must add that malware can be more or less lethal according to its target and to the aggressor's intent. An attack against critical infrastructure, for example, can be more or less lethal according to the type of structure and to the strength and length of the attack. The issue is therefore pending until we reach an international agreement, which, to date, is just desirable.

## Balance on and in Cyberspace

The Westphalia balance of power was dynamic. The substantial nuclear parity during the Cold War produced, instead, a static balance due to the certainty of a second strike through undetectable SMLBMs (Submarine-Launched Ballistic Missiles).

However, besides definition-related issues, the balance of power in cyberspace can hardly be attained for the following reasons[27]: the success of an attack depends more on defence quality than on the attack; the majority of offensive results come from civilian networks or from neutral and friendly States; due to the problems of identification of the goals of an attack, an

[27] A. Klimburg and L. Faesen, "A Balance of Power in Cyberspace", *European Cybersecurity Journal*, vol. 3, no. 4, 2018, p. 4.

escalation is more likely, all the more so because the offensive cyber weapons are cheap and user friendly, contrary to the defensive ones; cyber weapons can be used multiple times, but they can also become useless when vulnerabilities are patched; the cyberattack effects can be immediate or deferred, worsening or overturning traditional responses; the cyber weapons can be reverse engineered and used by the victim or by other subjects; the cyberattacks can jeopardise not only the target's security but sometimes also the security of other subjects with the same vulnerabilities; finally, cyberspace is full of stakeholders (mainly companies or individuals) with whom the State has to share decisions because of the technological nature of a system which is hard or impossible to overturn.

For these reasons, and for the ones that have already been mentioned, it is unlikely that the balance of power might be a stabilisation element in cyberspace, all the more so because nowadays the international system is witnessing a decreasing importance of the institutional, bureaucratic, and diplomatic tools, to the advantage of leading figures who take on decisions and behaviours for personal interests without considering medium and long-term consequences. In fact, the possibility of a rational calculation of balance through the mathematical game theory, which was plausible in the nuclear age, is unfeasible as well in the current system.

Only through a rearrangement of rules at the international level can we assume the feasibility of the balance of power theory for certain aspects of the conflict in the cyber domain, for example in the growing hybrid warfare sector, where both conventional and unconventional weapons are employed[28].

[28] A proposal for a definition of Hybrid Warfare is submitted in U. Gori, "Oltre l'ambiguità concettuale: significato e contenuti della Information Warfare, Cyber Warfare e Hybrid Cyber Warfare", in U. Gori (ed.), *Information, Cyber e Hybrid Warfare: contenuti, differenze, applicazioni*, Milan, FrancoAngeli, 2018, pp. 17-26. There is some empirical evidence that cyber weapons are effective only when used with kinetic ones. (See A. Craig and B. Valeriano, *Realism and Cyber Conflict: Security in the Digital Age*, 2018, available at www.E-IR.info). See also E. Gartzke

In other words, we need to re-establish the legitimating principles and system for the contemporary values shared by the majority of the great Powers, readapt the international law to the new reality and boost those regional tools, such as Confidence Building Measures (CBMs), that might reduce misinterpretation in cyberspace.

To date, attempts to issue a set of rules in cyberspace are limited to the Budapest Convention of 2001, the first international treaty on Internet crimes, the Tallin Manual and its 2.0 development, and the Wassenaar Arrangement.

So far, the diplomatic approach of establishing a voluntary set of rules through international organisations like the UN seems more viable than the establishment of legally binding rules, also because of unresolved definition issues for key concepts, in addition to the fact that the subjects are not just the States, but also IT industries and individuals[29].

It is therefore important to distinguish between power on cyberspace and power in cyberspace: right now, Internet governance is experiencing a power balance, mainly due to the technological nature of the cyber domain. However, as stated by the authors cited in footnote[30], "the conditions of an equilibrium of forces that lies at the core of the balance of power theory is currently impossible to establish as it requires States to have a basic understanding of each other capabilities, and therefore a minimum amount of agreed definitions as to what constitutes a 'cyberweapon'".

Furthermore, it is necessary to consider possible – and already planned – future developments. DARPA (Defense Advanced Research Projects Agency) is, for example, working on an automatic pre-programming cyberwar system[31], that is, a system

---

and J.R. Lindsay, "Thermonuclear Cyberwarfare", *Journal of Cyber Security*, vol.3, no. 1, 2017, pp. 37-48.

[29] See U. Gori, "Le nuove minacce cyber", in "Lo spazio cibernetico tra esigenze di sicurezza nazionale e tutela delle libertà individuali", *Informazioni della Difesa*, CSII-ISPRI, no. 6/2014, pp. 28-29.

[30] A. Klimburg and L. Faesen (2018), p. 4.

[31] On artificial intelligence see K. Suter, *AI can change the Balance of Power, Berlin*

without a human input: useful indeed in a zero-day attack case, but extremely dangerous, at this time, as the world's future is controlled by machines[32].

As we can see, the answer to the title's question, that is, whether a balance of power in the cyber age is feasible, is "no". Once again, technology has proved to be the crucial element for the world power set up.

---

*Policy Journal*, 2018. See also M. Caligiuri, *Intelligenza artificiale e ordine mondiale,* Gnosis, 1, 2018, pp. 55-65. But other problems are at the horizon: the properties of quantum mechanics defined "spooky" and unbelievable by Einstein, (entanglement, superposition (0+1), etc.) are now used to construct a new gneration of computers which will be able to crack everything, including the most sophisticate cryptographic tools, and perform in seconds computations which would take millions of years if made by normal devices. The development of this technological 'weapon' will dramatically modify the balance of power both in political and economic domain. V. Wadhwa, *Quantum Computing Is About To Overturn Cybersecurity's Balance Of Power*, Huffpost, 5 December 2015.

[32] The uncertain future of the distribution of power coupled with the technological threats on the rise lead to reflect on Willy Brandt's statement in a speech at Oslo University in 1971: "Ich begreife eine Politik fuer den Frieden als wahre Realpolitik dieser Epoche".

# 7. Defining Rules of Behaviour for Force and Coercion in Cyberspace

James A. Lewis

Permissible behaviour in cyberspace will initially be defined by the uniform and consistent practice of states. These practices by states are not yet distinct, and it is an open question as to the extent to which permissible behaviour can defined in the absence of experience. International conventions and treaties (such as the Hague and Geneva Conventions) were drafted and agreed upon after the experience of war and new technologies. We have not yet had this for cyberspace. However, certain trends can be identified by looking at what states do and where they feel constrained (noting that there are very few constraints when it comes to conflict in cyberspace).

Cyber operations and techniques are a new way to exercise power. Cyber may be best seen as an addition to the existing portfolio of coercive tools available to states, one which they have not been reluctant to use. How a state will use cyber techniques is determined by its larger interests, strategies, experience, and institutions, and its willingness to accept the risk of discovery and retaliation. In the current environment, since there is no real penalty for discovery, there is little incentive for any state to give up this new tool.

However, there is an implicit threshold (roughly determined by a state's view on what can be considered the use of force) that shapes state behaviour. Only a handful of cyber actions have crossed this line. States generally avoid actions that could justify damaging retaliation by the "victim". The use of force in cyberspace is also constrained, at least in confrontations between nuclear power, by the threat of escalation. Below this imprecise threshold, no other cyber action is constrained by anything other than a state's self-interest. In the current circumstances of international politics, the assertion in the Melian Dialogue that "the strong do what they can and the weak suffer what they must" remains particularly relevant.

This "force" threshold is imprecise, but states do not wish for an exact definition of the use of force, preferring a degree of ambiguity that creates space for national judgments attuned to political realities. International agreement on state behaviour reflects this deference to political judgment.

Progress towards a more stable and less dangerous cyberspace requires two steps: first, the further development of norms for responsible state behaviour that expand and make explicit the application of existing international law and state practice to cyber conflict (and there has been some progress towards this in the United Nations), and second, meaningful consequences for states that ignore these norms.

## The West Is on the Defensive

We live in a period of increasing conflict. International relations are being reshaped by several factors, including what some call a transfer of power from a Transatlantic to an Asian centre of gravity. Related to this transfer, the liberal western values that have guided state practice in conflict are eroding. American actions in Iraq and in cyber espionage accelerate the erosion and undercut the legitimacy of the post-1945 order. There is a broad discontent with the international *status quo* in many countries.

The institutions and rules created after 1945 are also being tested by powerful political forces as newly powerful states and a revanchist Russia pursue their own interests. Although the intellectual foundations of communism were destroyed with the end of the Cold War, the state institutions it had created were not. The former communist powers Russia and China (loosely aligned with Iran and North Korea) intend to disrupt (and, in China's case, restructure) the existing international order. Some of these challenges will eventually subside, but the next decade will be tumultuous.

These political forces change the nature of conflict and of permissible behaviour. Western concepts of permissible or responsible behaviour are shaped by the importance given to individuals rights, democratic institutions, and the rule of law. Rights, institutions, and law constrain the use of force within a state and the use of force between states. But as western institutions and norms are weakened, the risk of conflict will increase. The concepts and institutions developed by western nations in response to the global crises of the 1930s are no longer adequate. They do not reflect the distribution of global power. While the alternatives to the 1945 international order are unattractive – untrammelled authoritarian sovereigns or nebulous multistakeholder governance –, the *status quo* is no longer sufficient, and stability will be diminished until some model of international governance emerges that accommodates both a new balance of power and the changes created by information technologies.

The resurgence of nationalism and sovereignty sharpens conflict in cyberspace. Sovereignty is the antithesis of the "one world, no borders" approach of Internet visionaries. The growth of nationalism, which is in good measure a reaction to a Pax Americana world and US-led globalisation that emerged after 1990, accelerates this decline. The millennial vision that the end of the Cold War heralded the arrival of a world that would look largely like the United States, where borders were erased by technology and governments replaced by some mix of unelected stakeholders, is an artifact and no longer useful for guiding policy.

Non-interference in internal affairs was the norm for state behaviour before 1945. Since 1945, states have ceded some of their sovereign authority and accepted that there are issues, such as human rights, that transcend borders. This was the norm, but it is now challenged. Russia is not the only country to object to these agreements. It is joined in varying degrees by other newly influential states who seek to expand their international a role and do not necessarily share the experiences of war that led to the creation of "universal" values they often see as overly western.

Some nations would prefer to return to a more traditional world where sovereign rights take precedence and universal values are less important. Russia and China are among the most vociferous in objecting to intrusions into the internal affairs, yet their efforts run counter to powerful economic and political forces created by digital networks. If the old "one world" concept is inadequate, the effect of these forces makes efforts to return to the XIX century balance of powers equally inadequate.

The nature of warfare is being reshaped by new technologies, but above all, by nuclear weapons. Nuclear weapons make conflict among the nuclear powers too risky; and the increased sophistication and destructiveness of advanced conventional weapons, which can produce strategic effects without the use of nuclear weapons, impose a similar constraint. In this new period of interstate conflict, nations will seek new tools and techniques for coercion, to compel other states to take actions they would not otherwise choose. Cyber operations are ideal for this new kind of conflict.

Competition and conflict among great powers have been reshaped by information technologies. Cyberspace has become the primary battleground for the conflict between sovereignty and universal values, and between democracies and authoritarians. Until these conflicts are resolved, we should expect continued turmoil that will limit the scope of global consensus on norms.

Increasing conflict and competition form the unwelcome backdrop for a discussion of what is permissible behaviour by states in cyberspace. Conflict erodes the value of norms. The end of the Cold War was only a temporary triumph for market democracy and western liberalism. As a leading Chinese scholar put it, "We are moving away from a state in which international norms are led by Western liberalism to a state where international norms are no longer respected"[1]. There is a general discontent with the ideas once thought to embody progress, and this affects the effectiveness of norms, an effect accelerated by a nationalist reaction to the globalisation that surged at the end of the Cold War. This discontent and accompanying nationalism complicate policy-making in democracies.

It would be misleading to call this a new cold war, however. In the cold war, there was a clear demarcation between East and West that no longer exists. International relations are today defined by a high degree of openness and economic interconnections. While these connections do not guarantee peace any more than an earlier phase of globalisation did in 1914, they shape economic and social interactions in ways that are difficult for a single nation to manage or control without some degree of cooperation.

How this cooperation should be structured is in contention. Competing institutions, such as the BRICs, have appeared. While feeble, they reflect a larger debate. The last decade has seen the international community dispute the balance between traditional notions of national sovereignty and the universal values reflected in international commitments. Since 2000, there has been a reaction in some countries to the ascendance of universal rights. There has been a resurgence of the older notion of national sovereignty, which can be encapsulated as saying that a state has the right to do what it wants without interference in its own territory. The nexus of strategic competition is over how the world will be ordered and who will order it.

---

[1] http://chinamediaproject.org/2018/06/26yan-xuetong-on-the-bipolar-state-of-our-world/

## An Ill-Governed Space

From the start, cyberspace has been loosely governed. This was by design and made sense for the 1990s, when conflict seemed unlikely, and for the fledgling technology, which benefitted from an absence of constraints, but this ad hoc, laissez-faire approach has created unacceptable risks. Cyberspace provides unprecedented economic and social benefits, but with these came real threats to international security. Powerful nations see it as an unconstrained arena for conflict, and dangerous actions by State and non-State actors have produced a growing sense of concern in the international community.

These concerns have created global demand for better and more explicit governance structures for what has become an essential global infrastructure. Governance describes how individuals and both public and private institutions manage shared interests and responsibilities. It can include both informal arrangements and formal institutions. Norms are foundational for better governance. A norm is an expectation for appropriate behaviour. A norm works best when the international community is seized by it, when it shapes the behaviour of public and private institutions and the decisions of national leaders, and when it makes clear to all that some actions fall outside the bounds of what is acceptable.

## Cyber Operations

Cyber operations are ideal for achieving coercive and strategic effects in this environment. Cyber operations offer capabilities that are well suited for the new political-military environment. Cyber capabilities create an operational space in which nations can conduct offensive actions with less political risk, given the "gray areas" in international law, created by the limits of applying laws written for the physical world to cyberspace. Cyber conflicts inhabit this gray zone, since it can complicate the ability of opponents to respond to hostile actions. Cyber-attacks and the effects produced by the manipulation of software, data, knowledge, and opinion create a new operational space for force and coercive action. The operational effect of military cyber operations will be to degrade the performance of political decision-makers, commanders, troops, and weapons, while the strategic effect will be to diminish the opponent's will and capacity to resist.

We are in a period of experimentation where, as in the 1930s with tanks, aircraft, and aircraft carriers, nations tested how to use the new technologies to gain military advantage. Just as tanks and planes reshaped warfare, new technologies are changing warfare in this century. These technologies include unmanned, robotic platforms, hypersonic strike vehicles, space and anti-satellite weapons, precision-guided weapons, and cyber operations. Should there be armed conflict among major states, we can expect to see cyber-attacks combined with electronic warfare, antisatellite attacks, informational campaigns, and other unconventional tactics and weapons. But countries will seek to avoid such clashes. In the state of persistent "non-kinetic" conflict we find ourselves in today, the emphasis will be on gaining intelligence advantage, on exerting coercive effect and opinion shaping.

International understandings that can lead to norms on the use of cyber operations will require reconceptualising the idea of the use of force. States no longer need to rely on kinetic or conventional means to exercise force or achieve coercive effects. There is an unexpected congruence between the norms for human rights, particularly freedom of expression, and the norms for warfare. How should we constraint the ability of nations to use freedom of speech exercised over Internet-enabled social networks as a coercive tool? This was not something envisioned by either the Hague or Geneva convention.

The discussion of cyber's role in this new kind of conflict is distorted by the classical strategic thought on nuclear weapons. Nuclear war threatened catastrophe. A catastrophic cyber-attack is, however, very unlikely. A major cyber-attack will not produce a crippling blow and might only enrage a nuclear-armed opponent. The risk is not worth the result. In this context, the value of a discussion on "strategic stability" is open to question. Strategic stability is an inheritance from nuclear war, from a time when a miscalculation could lead to devasting consequences within minutes. This is not the case with cyber operations. If stability means there is no incentive for a nation to use force to improve its position *vis-à-vis* opponents, we are well past this point in the relations among contending states.

The Internet changes how people think and interact. It has a measurable effect on politics and the legitimacy of a state with its own population. Efforts to create cognitive effects for coercive purposes has changed the nature of interstate conflicts. Cognitive effects have implications for military operations and interstate relations and may be more important than using cyber operations to achieve kinetic effects. As one America General put it, "the mind is the new battlefield".

Cyber operations provide a new way to achieve military and strategic advantage, but this will not come from some virtual equivalent of a nuclear catastrophe or strategic bombing. The objective in this new kind of conflict is not destruction (which cyber operations are not well suited for), but cognitive effects, the manipulation of information to change thoughts and behaviours. In essence, the strategic goal is to damage morale, cohesion, political stability, with the goal of ultimately diminishing the opponent's will to resist. Cyber operations allow an attacker to manipulate information and opinion in ways that have a coercive or disruptive effect, without the risk of open warfare and while staying below the threshold of "use of force." While all non-democratic opponents (Russia, Iran, China, and North Korea) have experimented with using cyber operations to produce cognitive effects and control their own domestic populations, Russia has succeeded first in developing advanced techniques and capabilities. China and Iran, looking at the Russian successes against western countries, are studying how to emulate it.

One benefit of cyber operations is that coercive actions can be taken while minimising the risk of escalation. In contemplating the use of cyber operations, one factor that weighs upon all opponents is the immense capacity of the United States to inflict punishment, and judging from their behaviour, Russia, China, Iran, and North Korea have strategies to minimise or avoid the risk of retaliation while still using coercion to achieve their ends. They weigh the benefits from cyber operations against the risk of escalation and retaliation. Western nations should plan for increased use by our opponents of coercive acts that fall below implicit thresholds for the use of force or armed attack.

## Norms for Responsible State Behaviour in Cyberspace

In 1998, Russia proposed[2] that the UN develop "international principles that would enhance the security of global information and telecommunications systems and help to combat information terrorism and criminality". This proposal was the start of a long process of discussion among national representatives under the UN's Committee on Disarmament and International Security (the First Committee) in the Reports of the United Nations Group of Government Experts (GGE) on "Developments in the Field of Information and Telecommunications in the Context of International Security". The GGE's first report in 2010 created the international agenda for cybersecurity[3], as it called for the international community to undertake work to develop norms of responsible state

[2] United Nations, General Assembly, Resolution 53/70 - Developments in the field of information and telecommunications in the context of international security, A/RES/53/70, New York, 4 January 1999.

[3] A/65/201, Report of the Group of Governmental Experts on Developments in the Field of Information and Telecommunications in the Context of International Security.

behaviour and confidence-building measures and take action to build cybersecurity capability on a global basis.

The second round of UN GGE discussions in 2013 created the framework for norms and confidence-building measures as they apply to international cybersecurity. The 2013 Report[4] asserted that the UN Charter, international law, and the principles of state sovereignty applied to cyberspace. This agreement on the application of sovereignty and international law embedded cyberspace and cybersecurity in the existing framework of international relations and practices that govern conduct among states. It ended the idea of cyberspace as global commons without borders and began to lay out areas of state responsibility.

The 2013 Report was followed by another in 2015[5] which continued the development of norms, and which was endorsed by UN member states. The central conclusion of these Reports is that the UN Charter, International Law, and the principle of state sovereignty apply equally to state action in cyberspace as they do in the physical world. This is an important foundation step towards stability, but the GGE as a negotiating platform for defining responsible behaviour may have reached the end of its useful life, if only because many nations increasingly want a more inclusive and more formal venue for the global discussion of cybersecurity, and because it is now clear that the creation of norms for responsible state behaviour by themselves does not produce stability or security.

The 2015 Report revealed a fundamental dispute in the positions of nations regarding cyber warfare. Russian experts argue that cyber-attacks could produce an effect equivalent to a weapon of mass destruction and should be treated as such, i.e., stigmatised and banned. A precedent can be found in the Treaty

---

[4] A/68/98, Report of the Group of Governmental Experts on Developments in the Field of Information and Telecommunications in the Context of International Security.

[5] A/70/174, Report of the Group of Governmental Experts on Developments in the Field of Information and Telecommunications in the Context of International Security.

on the Peaceful Uses of Outer Space, where nations agree not to place weapons of mass destruction in space as well as to other constraints that limit space activities to peaceful purposes. The US position is that international agreements should embed the legitimate use of cyber-attack in the framework of international law, and accept that the use of cyber-attack is legitimate if guided by the principles of the laws of armed conflict that nations have agreed to follow.

The GGE norms did not address the use of social media or cyber techniques for politically coercive purposes. Some would point to the Arab Spring or the Colour Revolutions as examples of the use of such techniques to interfere in a country's internal affairs, but the most compelling case (before the 2016 hack and related leaks targeting the 2016 US presidential election) was Russia's use of proxy forces to launch low-level cyber-attacks against Estonia in 2007. Since that incident, Russian cyber warfare doctrine has evolved considerably. It emphasises the manipulation of public opinion for political effect. The Russians have been skillful at exploiting social media to achieve a "cognitive effect" (the older term was "reflexive control"). The interference in European and American politics in 2016 made clear that the battle for cyber is now in the mind, not in critical infrastructure.

Existing norms and confidence building measures (CBMs) do not directly address cognitive effect. Actions intended to produce a cognitive effect could be interpreted as violating the 2013 GGE commitment to respect the UN Charter and its requirement not to use force or threats of force to damage or threaten the political independence of a country[6], but no one would call what Russia has done a use of force. The grey areas in existing norms and internal law have been skillfully exploited by Russia and, as with the hybrid warfare seen in the intrusion into Ukraine, western nations have not yet developed an effective response, nor is there any platform for negotiations on how to constrain or punish these new kinds of coercive actions.

---

[6] In Article 2/4 of the Convention

The GGE has been hampered in considering such issues, as its charter precludes any discussion of espionage (thus putting the most frequent use of cyber operations by states like China or the US outside of consideration), human rights, which are routinely and mechanically endorsed in each report, or crime, which is considered the purview of other UN bodies. It may be that the usefulness of these negotiations has come to its end, but it is not clear what will replace the GGE.

Cybersecurity began as an all-encompassing concept, reflecting the rhetoric of the Internet community, but the decision now is whether to focus the international discussion on specific topics within the purview of specialised and appropriate groups – international law, crime, human rights. The task of defining norms is complicated by the lack of experience and open discussion in the use of cyber operations in conflict and by the efforts by states to innovate in developing new techniques for coercion.

## Action Establishes Boundaries and Norms

The UN Charter makes clear that any act by one state that threatens the territorial integrity, or the political independence, of another state is illegal, and could justify a punitive response. Russian cyber operations do not threaten territorial integrity, but they do threaten political independence. They are part of a larger Russian effort to shape politics in the West and to advance Russian foreign policy goals using misinformation, subsidies, and Internet trolls.

Russian attempts at manipulation do not signal the return of the Cold War. Russian tactics are different and require a different response. We are not going to war with Russia over hacking, nor will nuclear weapons deter it, but that does not mean inaction is the best choice. This is not the Cold War, but a new kind of conflict where the defence of democracy will require new concepts and tools that have yet to be developed.

One lesson that can be drawn from our experience with State-sponsored hacking is that if there is no response by the victim, an opponent will take this as a signal to continue. A major goal for international cybersecurity is to establish consequences for malicious action; since without consequences, malicious cyber actions will increase. Disputes over evidentiary standards miss the point. This is politics, not jurisprudence. The rules for international politics are not the same as those used in a court, and while a world where the Rule of Law dominates may be our goal, it is a goal that is currently growing more distant. Holding to a legal evidentiary standard only increases the likelihood of indecision and continued opponent action.

Nations need to respond to hostile cyber actions if we are to establish the boundaries of permissible behaviour in cyberspace. This leads to the more difficult question of defining an appropriate response, as the "weaponisation" of speech delivered by social media enabled by the Internet, is not a problem envisioned in the existing rules of armed conflict. The goal for policy should be to change this, building the precedents for attribution, response, and thresholds established by US actions against our other cyber opponents. Hacking should not be penalty free if we want it to stop.

The options for response include damaging counter-leaks about corruption or governmental indifference, indictments, sanctions, or some other public censure. Military action is risky, given Russia's confrontational attitude, but some limited military cyber operation, accompanied by an effective diplomatic strategy, may be necessary if we are to change the risk calculation of Russia and other opponents. Other options might include some kind of stricture on an attacker's Internet connectivity, but the ability to carry out this kind of action is not well developed.

The most immediate response is likely to use legal tools such as retorsion and countermeasures, such as sanctions or indictments. Since the evidentiary standards for imposing sanctions are lower than for indictments, they might be preferred.

Sanctions are also a more flexible tool than indictments, more visible than covert action, and they displease the Russians. All this makes them an attractive option, but after numerous sanctions, the behaviour of our four opponents has not changed. Sanctions are a good first step, but additional measures are necessary. The US and its allies need to consider whether to use cyber operation against Russia, perhaps similar to what Joint Task Force Ares was able to do against ISIS, but any military action would need to be carefully considered to ensure proportionality and to manage the risk of escalation. In the language of arms control, the US and its allies need to populate all the rungs of the deterrence ladder with appropriate and proportional responses to hostile acts.

The recent discovery that Russia hacked numerous US electrical power companies was most likely intended as a warning to the US not to retaliate – "what we did in Ukraine we can do to you...". The US would need to signal to Russia that further incidents or escalation will be more of a risk for Putin's regime than anything else. Ultimately, responding to Russian political operations against the West will require a larger strategy that recognises the end of the period of unchallenged American supremacy, repairing the alliance among democracies, and developing new kinds of responses to cyber actions, but a first step is not to let hacks go unpunished. To do otherwise will unravel any progress to make cyberspace more stable and secure.

A policy of response and retaliation will restore credibility and increase the incentives for opponents to negotiate. The parallels with earlier arms control precedents mean that there is the possibility for productive discussions even between hostile powers. Any agreement or institution will need to emerge from the interaction among states with different and competing interests – this is not 1945 when there was widespread consensus on the need for stabilising institutions, nor is it 1975, when Cold War opponents were ready to reach accommodations to increase stability.

We did not get an agreement on nuclear arms control and the entire panoply of non-proliferation agreements until after the Cuban missile crisis, when leading powers were frightened and convinced of the existential threat of nuclear weapons. Countries began to engage seriously and were willing to accept constraints. We have not faced an existential threat in cyberspace, nor is this likely in the near future. Since cyber operations rarely pose an immediate, existential threat, there will be less incentive to reach an agreement on constraints, but there is one area where international agreements among opponents could usefully be pursued. That would be to control and constrain the use of cyberattacks and ban some categories of attacks entirely. This is the area where the interests of opposing states are most likely to overlap.

Realistically, the absence of an agreed international framework for cybersecurity, accompanied by the increased international tensions and challenges to transatlantic leadership, limit the ability to reach an agreement anytime soon. The immediate focus for western policy should be on assembling like-minded nations to operationalise norms and consequences while continuing to explore whether a further agreement with opponents is possible at the margins of what was agreed in 2015. Progress requires finding some way to involve private actors. It also requires recognition of the central role of the UN. While many Americans discount the UN, other countries see it as the locus of international governance and a US strategy must take this into account. Precedents from other domains are of limited value for cybersecurity. We need ideas that recognise the world as it is, conflictive and dominated by states, and not as we imagined it when the United States was unchallenged.

# The Authors

**Dean Cheng** is a Senior Research Fellow for Chinese Political and Military Affairs at the Heritage Foundation, after working at the Center for Naval Analysis, SAIC, and the US Congress Office of Technology Assessment. He is a long-time observer of China's military, with a particular interest in China's space programme and Chinese military doctrine. He has testified before Congress, and spoken at various institutions, including MIT and the US National Defense University. He is the author of *Cyber Dragon: Inside China's Information Warfare and Cyber Operations* (2016).

**Umberto Gori** is Professor Emeritus at the University of Florence. From 1975 to 2007 he was Full Professor of International Relations and Strategic Studies at the "Cesare Alfieri" Faculty of Political Sciences. He is President of the interdepartmental Center of Strategic, International and Entrepreneurial Studies (CSSII), and Professor at the Naval Academy, Italian Navy, and the School of Air War, Air Force. Dr. Gori has been also a Lecturer at the Diplomatic Institute, Italian Ministry of Foreign Affairs. He was Visiting Professor in French, German and US Universities. Author, or editor, of 30 books, and more than 200 publications. He received his PhD in International Organization.

**Garrett Hinck** is a James C. Gaither Junior Fellow for the Cyber Policy Initiative and Nuclear Policy Program at the

Carnegie Endowment for International Peace. He is a graduate of the Walsh School of Foreign Service at Georgetown University with a degree in Science, Technology and International Affairs. He has written on cybersecurity and international law for Lawfare, where he was previously an intern at the Brookings Institution.

**James A. Lewis** is a Senior Fellow and Programme Director at the Center for Strategic and International Studies (CSIS). Before joining CSIS, he worked at the Departments of State and Commerce. He was the Advisor for the 2010, 2013 and 2015 United Nations Group of Governmental Experts on Information Security and led a long-running Track II dialogue on cybersecurity with the China Institute of Contemporary International Relations. Dr. Lewis has authored many publications and is an internationally recognised expert on cybersecurity. He has testified numerous times before Congress and is frequently quoted in the media. Lewis received his PhD from the University of Chicago.

**Tim Maurer** is Co-Director of the Cyber Policy Initiative at the Carnegie Endowment for International Peace. Since 2010, his work has been focusing on cybersecurity, human rights in the digital age, and Internet governance, currently with a specific focus on cybersecurity and financial stability. He has been a member of several US track 1.5 cyber dialogues and involved in the Global Commission on the Stability of Cyberspace, the Freedom Online Coalition's working group "An Internet Free and Secure", and the Global Commission on Internet Governance. He his author of *Cyber Mercenaries: The State, Hackers, and Power, a comprehensive study examining proxy relationships between states and hackers* (2018).

**Fabio Rugge**, Counselor, is Head of ISPI's Centre on Cybersecurity, promoted in partnership with Leonardo. He is a diplomat currently working at Fincantieri as Senior Advisor to the President for International and Institutional Affairs. From 2012 to 2016 he worked at the Italian Prime Minister's Office and prior to that he was Counselor at the Italian Delegation to the North Atlantic Council in Brussels and Consul General of Italy in Mumbai (India). He held several positions at the Ministry of Foreign Affairs and International Cooperation in Rome – among others at the Policy Planning Unit and as Head of the Office in charge for scholarships and the internationalisation of Italian Universities. Since 2013, Fabio Rugge is Adjunct Professor of Security Studies at the University of Florence. He held courses in several Italian Universities (LUISS, Sant'Anna, Link Campus, Tor Vergata) on Cybersecurity and International Relations.

**Daniel A. Pinkston** is a Lecturer in International Relations with Troy University. Previously he was the Northeast Asia Deputy Project Director for the International Crisis Group in Seoul, and the Director of the East Asia Nonproliferation Program at the James Martin Center for Nonproliferation Studies. Dr. Pinkston received his PhD in International Affairs from the University of California, San Diego, and he has a master's degree in Korean Studies from Yonsei University. He is the author of *The North Korean Ballistic Missile Program*, and has published several scholarly articles on Korean security affairs. He also served as a Korean linguist in the US Air Force.

**Lior Tabansky** is a Scholar of Cyber Power at Tel Aviv University's Blavatnik Interdisciplinary Cyber Research Center. His current research interests are: national innovation systems and capacity building; hostile influence operations via social media; comparative defence adaptation. Dr. Lior's doctoral dissertation "Explaining National Cyber Insecurity: A New Strategic Defense Adaptation Analytical Framework" (Tel Aviv University, School of Government and Politics) explains why even the most developed nations remain so exposed to destructive cyberattacks on strategic homeland targets by foreign states. He co-authored *Cybersecurity in Israel* (2015) with Professor Isaac Ben-Israel the first comprehensive "insider" account of Israeli policy and operations.

CPSIA information can be obtained
at www.ICGtesting.com
Printed in the USA
LVHW080601230123
737748LV00017B/277

9 788867 058655